Supercharge
Your
MEMORY

Supercharge
Your
MEMORY

More than 100 Exercises
to Energize Your Mind

Corinne L. Gediman &
Francis M. Crinella, Ph.D.

STERLING

New York / London
www.sterlingpublishing.com

Acknowledgments

A special thank you to the following folks for making this book possible:
Coleen O'Shea and Marilyn Allen, our literary agents Meredith Peters Hale, Rodman Pilgrim Neumann and the entire supportive staff at Sterling Publishing Co., Inc.
Barry Gediman and Julie Paige for their support and wisdom.

STERLING and the distinctive Sterling logo are registered trademarks of Sterling Publishing Co., Inc.

Library of Congress Cataloging-in-Publication Data

Gediman, Corinne, 1949-
  Supercharge your memory! : more than 100 exercises to energize your mind / Corinne L. Gediman and Francis M. Crinella.
    p. cm.
  Includes bibliographical references and index.
  ISBN-13: 978-1-4027-4355-9
  ISBN-10: 1-4027-4355-6
  1. Mnemonics. 2. Memory. 3. Intellect—Problems, exercises, etc. I. Crinella, Francis M. II. Title.

BF385.G44 2008
153.1´4—dc22

                        2007033413

10   9   8   7   6   5   4   3   2   1

Published by Sterling Publishing Co., Inc.
387 Park Avenue South, New York, NY 10016
Text © 2008 by Corinne L. Gediman and Francis M. Crinella, Ph.D.
Illustrations © 2008 by Gilbert Ford
Distributed in Canada by Sterling Publishing
^c/o Canadian Manda Group, 165 Dufferin Street
Toronto, Ontario, Canada M6K 3H6
Distributed in the United Kingdom by GMC Distribution Services
Castle Place, 166 High Street, Lewes, East Sussex, England BN7 1XU
Distributed in Australia by Capricorn Link (Australia) Pty. Ltd.
P.O. Box 704, Windsor, NSW 2756, Australia

Book Design: Rachel Maloney
Illustrated by: Gilbert Ford
Photo Credits are listed on page 150.

Printed in China
All rights reserved

Sterling ISBN-13: 978-1-4027-4335-9
        ISBN-10: 1-4027-4335-6

For information about custom editions, special sales, premium and
corporate purchases, please contact Sterling Special Sales
Department at 800-805-5489 or specialsales@sterlingpublishing.com.

Contents

Getting Started

There is an abundance of tools available today to help us remember. They range from sophisticated electronic devices such as Palm Pilots, BlackBerrys, and laptop computers to more traditional devices such as diary systems, paper-based calendars, and Post-it notes. Additionally, we have electronic locators to help us track down missing objects, such as our car in a crowded parking lot. So why bother with improving our natural memory? It is true that these devices can help us to be less forgetful and more organized in our daily lives, but they are not a substitute for a robust and reliable natural memory.

The human brain is more powerful and more important than any computer in existence. Without brain-powered memory we would not be able to learn anything new. Without brain-powered memory we would not be able to reminisce about the past or engage in conversation. As we live longer, we need our brains to function longer than did those of the generation before us. What can we do to offset the natural brain aging process that begins in our late twenties?

Can memory be improved? There are many ways to improve memory and offset natural memory decline as we age. Memory can be trained to be more efficient and reliable. Memory works by attention and association. First you must pay attention. You can't remember—and you certainly can't improve your memory—if you don't pay attention and focus in the moment. Second, memory works by association. Association is the process of linking new memories to information the brain already knows. These linkages serve as memory hooks, boosting information storage and retrieval. The more you learn, the greater your associative powers. We can train our brains to use association techniques to create a better memory.

Exercising your mind and memory can literally build a better brain. Cutting-edge research demonstrates that the brain is a dynamic organ capable of regeneration. When stimulated, brain cells wake up and start talking to one another. As a result, communication pathways among brain cells have been shown to increase in number and complexity, and new brain cells have been spotted in the area of the hippocampus, the brain's center for new learning and memory. A more active brain is a more robust brain, and a more robust brain provides protection against senility.

In *Supercharge Your Memory!* you will take back control of your natural memory by learning and practicing memory-boosting techniques in a series of fun and fast-paced memory games and exercises in six lessons. As you progress through these brain-stimulating exercises, you will be building a better memory and a better brain.

Supercharge Your Memory! offers the dual benefit of fun and functionality. On the one hand, it's chock-full of engaging memory games you can play alone or with friends and family. On the other, it's also a practical, research-based memory-improvement program, proven to boost memory at any age.

As you progress through this book, you'll complete six lessons, each one building on the others to help you develop important memory skills. Before we begin, let's take a look at the science behind each lesson and the memory gains you'll achieve.

Program Overview
Lesson One, "Thanks for the Memories"

Scientifically Speaking: One of our greatest fears as we age is the fear of significant memory loss. Luckily most of us will experience only a minor and gradual decline in some short-term memory functionality that, while frustrating, will not interfere with our ability to live full and functional lives. It is estimated that Alzheimer's disease, the most dreaded form of senility, affects 10 percent of people over age sixty-five and 50 percent of people over age eighty-five. Healthy lifestyle choices, including brain exercises, can help slow down and ward off diseases of the brain that lead to senility.

Using advanced brain-imaging technology, neuroscientists now know that memory power peaks at around the age of thirty. They also know that the brain is a dynamic organ capable of rebuilding and regenerating itself. "Use it or lose it" applies not just to building and preserving muscle mass, but also to building and preserving memory and mental agility. It is easier to start preserving your memory now than to try to regain it as the years go by. But it's never too late; anyone, at any age, can benefit from these exercises.

What You'll Learn: Motivation is key to pursuing any program of improvement. Lesson One boosts motivation by engaging you in a series of games and exercises that cause you to reflect on just how important your memory is. As you participate in the games and exercises, you will literally be lighting up portions of your brain associated with *episodic memories*. Episodic memories are long-term memories of things you've personally experienced that make up the fabric of your life and contribute to who you are. At the end of the lesson, you'll be presented with easy follow-up actions you can take to strengthen your episodic memory and build a treasure trove of cherished memories.

Lesson Two, "Your Learning Style"

Scientifically Speaking: Learning and memory are two sides of the same coin. In order to remember something, we must first learn it. Each of us has a preferred way of learning that scientists refer to as a *learning style*. There are three primary learning styles: visual (learning by seeing), auditory (learning by hearing), and experiential (learning by doing). In the general population, 65 percent of adults are visual learners, 30 percent of adults are auditory learners, and 5 percent of adults are experiential learners.

What You'll Learn: Understanding your unique learning style can help you select the most effective internal and external memory techniques for you. When you do this, you create a personalized approach to boosting memory. As you participate in the exciting games and exercises in Lesson Two, you will

identify your personal learning style and understand how to apply it to improving your memory. At the end of Lesson Two, you'll be presented with follow-up actions you can take to leverage your learning style in various memory situations.

Lesson Three, "Working Memories Made Easy," and Lesson Four, "Long-term Memories That Last"

Scientifically Speaking: Most people think of memory as an all-or-nothing function. In fact, memory is a series of processes, all of which must function well together in order for memories to be made, stored, and retrieved. Not all memories are stored in the same place. For instance, scientists believe that memories of faces and those of the names that go with them are stored at different locations in the brain. Also, some memories have more staying power than others. Memories that have a personal or emotional association have greater sticking power than those that do not. If you want to strengthen the anatomy of your body, it helps to understand the location and function of the major muscle groups. Likewise, if you want to improve your memory, it helps to understand memory processes. This way, you can align your memory-improvement strategies and learning styles with your brain's own memory-making processes.

What You'll Learn: In Lessons Three and Four, you will learn how the brain makes memories. You'll understand how memories begin as *sensory perceptions* that link to your learning style. These sensory perceptions include sight (visual learner), sound (auditory learner), and touch (experiential learner), as well as taste and smell. You'll also see how sensory perceptions are converted into working memories, and how select working memories are converted into long-term memories. Through a series of dynamic games, you'll activate and strengthen your brain's working memory and long-term memory processes. You'll also get tips on how to use your learning style to boost these two important memory functions. At the end of each lesson, you'll be presented with follow-up actions you can take to improve your memory.

Lesson Five, "Attention, Please!" and Lesson Six, "Make an Association"

Scientifically Speaking: All memory-boosting techniques are based on two fundamental principles that are the result of extensive memory research. The first principle is *attention*. You can't remember what you don't pay attention to in the first place. A significant percentage of memory complaints turn out to be the result of not being mentally present in the moment when the information was to be learned. The second principle is *association*. All memories are based on association, whether conscious or unconscious. By consciously choosing to create associations between what you want to remember and what your brain already knows, you form strong memory hooks by which to store and later retrieve important memories. Understanding how these two memory principles work together can help you achieve an A+ recall.

What You'll Learn: In Lessons Five and Six, you'll engage in a series of fast and fun games designed to boost your skills with regard to the important memory principles of attention and association. You'll also get an opportunity to apply your learning style to boost attention and association. At the end of these lessons, you'll be presented with follow-up actions you can take to sharpen your attention and association skills, putting you on the path to achieving an A+ memory.

Tools for Success

To help you take full advantage of each lesson in the book, we have created four learning tools: game headers, memory boosters, memory assessments, and memory chargers.

Game Headers: Game headers identify the memory skills and processes used in each game—as well as the corresponding challenge level, indicated by a color-coded bar that ranges from green to yellow to orange to red, where green is least challenging and red is most challenging.

Memory Boosters: Memory boosters are information boxes containing tips and techniques for boosting your memory success in the game at hand. Where appropriate, memory boosters include tips for how to use your preferred learning style in the game. Be sure to read the Memory Booster before beginning the exercise.

Memory Assessment: Memory assessments are simple self-assessment tools to help you rate your memory skill level after completing an exercise.

Memory Chargers: Memory chargers are fun follow-up actions you can take to reinforce each memory lesson in your everyday life.

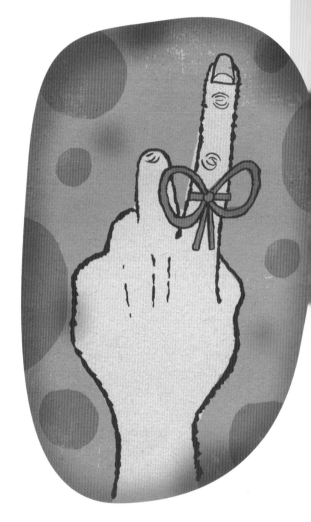

Thanks for the Memories

Life is all memory, except for the one present moment that goes by you
so quickly you hardly catch it going.

—Tennessee Williams

How Important Is Memory?

Imagine for a moment what your life would be like if you didn't have memories. Each moment would be unconnected to the next. Today's experiences would be singular events without context. Decisions would be random, based on intuition rather than experience. New learning could not be retained or recalled. People you met today would be forgotten tomorrow. Your world would be a series of fleeting sensory perceptions without context.

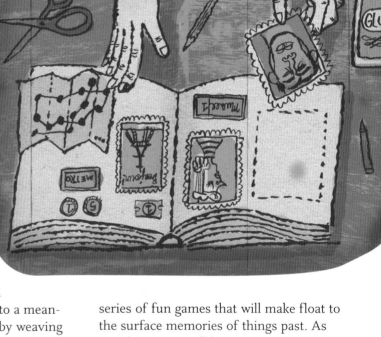

So how important is memory? Memory is the critical brain function that connects us to a meaningful life. It forms our identity by weaving together our thoughts, feelings, experiences, and relationships. Memory is the foundation of thinking that enables us to use stored information to compare, evaluate, imagine, and make decisions.

We fill our photo albums, journals, diaries, and scrapbooks with memories in an effort to save and recall cherished moments. In Lesson One, you'll open your brain's personal memory scrapbook as you engage in a series of fun games that will make float to the surface memories of things past. As you do so, you will be exercising and strengthening your brain's episodic memory functions.

Remember, episodic memories are memories of personally experienced places, events, and people. As we age, this memory function actually strengthens, allowing us to recall cherished memories of the special people and events in our lives.

When I Was Young

How to Play

Respond to each of the following questions with a colorful childhood memory. Turn this exercise into a game. Invite your family or friends to play along. One person reads the question. Everyone writes down responses. When all the questions have been read and answered, share your responses. What new things did you learn about one another? What additional childhood memories were triggered?

1. What was the name of your favorite teacher in elementary school?
2. Who was your first romantic heartthrob?
3. What school subject excited you the most?
4. What school subject gave you a stomachache?
5. What movie star did you have a crush on?
6. What is the first birthday party you remember?
7. What was the bravest thing you did as a child?
8. Who was your first real childhood friend?
9. What pop singer or singing group did you think was extra trendy in high school?
10. What is your proudest childhood moment?
11. What was your favorite board game as a kid?
12. What was your greatest childhood challenge?
13. With whom did you share your secrets?
14. What was your favorite childhood storybook?
15. What did you want to be when you grew up?
16. Describe a room in your home where your family gathered.
17. What was the first TV show you remember watching?
18. Where were you when you lost your first tooth?
19. What was your favorite Halloween costume?
20. What was your favorite ice cream on a stick?
21. Who taught you about the "birds and the bees"?
22. Describe an outdoor game the kids in your neighborhood played.
23. What was the worst illness you had as a child?
24. What childhood toy did you hang onto the longest?
25. What physical feature did you like most about yourself as a kid? What physical feature did you like least?
26. What was the best summer vacation you ever had as a kid?
27. What was considered trendy attire when you were in high school?
28. What was the address of your childhood home?
29. What was your favorite food?
30. Who taught you how to ride a two-wheeler bike?
31. What was your first pet's name?
32. What trinket from your childhood is still in your possession?
33. What were your high school's official colors?
34. Who was your childhood hero/heroine?
35. If you could relive a moment from your childhood, what would it be?

When I Say . . . You Think . . .

When I say candy you think Halloween.

How to Play

Fill in each sentence with a word or image that has a strong and specific personal memory for you. Go with your first impression. Turn this exercise into a fun family game. One person reads the questions out loud. Everyone writes down his or her first thought. At the end, compare your responses.

1. When I say animal, you think . . .
2. When I say love, you think . . .
3. When I say sport, you think . . .
4. When I say summer, you think . . .
5. When I say school, you think . . .
6. When I say city, you think . . .
7. When I say danger, you think . . .
8. When I say travel, you think . . .
9. When I say soldier, you think . . .
10. When I say dream, you think . . .
11. When I say spooky, you think . . .
12. When I say pleasure, you think . . .
13. When I say country, you think . . .
14. When I say holiday, you think . . .
15. When I say water, you think . . .
16. When I say popcorn, you think . . .
17. When I say tease, you think . . .
18. When I say nickname, you think . . .
19. When I say penny, you think . . .
20. When I say guilty, you think . . .
21. When I say honesty, you think . . .
22. When I say trouble, you think . . .
23. When I say food, you think . . .
24. When I say song, you think . . .
25. When I say memory, you think . . .
26. When I say magic, you think . . .
27. When I say cool, you think . . .
28. When I say dance, you think . . .
29. When I say homemade, you think . . .
30. When I say star, you think . . .
31. When I say helpful, you think . . .
32. When I say special friend, you think . . .
33. When I say yesterday, you think . . .
34. When I say movie, you think . . .
35. When I say beach, you think . . .
36. When I say game, you think . . .
37. When I say hunt, you think . . .
38. When I say borrow, you think . . .
39. When I say tomorrow, you think . . .
40. When I say family, you think . . .

Bloodhound

How to Play

Smells can trigger long-forgotten memories. Through research on mice, scientists believe that humans have about a thousand sensory receptors in their noses and can identify about ten thousand different odors. Initially, all smells are perceived as neutral. However, personal exposure causes us to remember smells as pleasant, unpleasant, or neutral. Categorize each smell below as pleasant, unpleasant, or neutral. Then recall a personal memory associated with each smell. Become a bloodhound by trying to experience the world through your olfactory senses. You'll be surprised at the memories your sense of smell can trigger.

fresh-cut grass
- [ ] pleasant
- [ ] unpleasant
- [ ] neutral

skunk
- [ ] pleasant
- [ ] unpleasant
- [ ] neutral

fireplace smoke
- [ ] pleasant
- [ ] unpleasant
- [ ] neutral

wine
- [ ] pleasant
- [ ] unpleasant
- [ ] neutral

roses
- [ ] pleasant
- [ ] unpleasant
- [ ] neutral

dog fur
- [ ] pleasant
- [ ] unpleasant
- [ ] neutral

baby powder
- [ ] pleasant
- [ ] unpleasant
- [ ] neutral

popcorn
- [ ] pleasant
- [ ] unpleasant
- [ ] neutral

pine needles
- [ ] pleasant
- [ ] unpleasant
- [ ] neutral

cinnamon
- [ ] pleasant
- [ ] unpleasant
- [ ] neutral

salty ocean air
- [ ] pleasant
- [ ] unpleasant
- [ ] neutral

horse or cow manure
- [ ] pleasant
- [ ] unpleasant
- [ ] neutral

fresh-baked bread
- [ ] pleasant
- [ ] unpleasant
- [ ] neutral

fresh paint
- [ ] pleasant
- [ ] unpleasant
- [ ] neutral

disinfectant sprays
- [ ] pleasant
- [ ] unpleasant
- [ ] neutral

sweaty locker room
- [ ] pleasant
- [ ] unpleasant
- [ ] neutral

cigarette smoke
- [ ] pleasant
- [ ] unpleasant
- [ ] neutral

old, musty antiques
- [ ] pleasant
- [ ] unpleasant
- [ ] neutral

dentist's office
- [ ] pleasant
- [ ] unpleasant
- [ ] neutral

bath soaps
- [ ] pleasant
- [ ] unpleasant
- [ ] neutral

calamine lotion
- [ ] pleasant
- [ ] unpleasant
- [ ] neutral

scented candles
- [ ] pleasant
- [ ] unpleasant
- [ ] neutral

coffee brewing
- [ ] pleasant
- [ ] unpleasant
- [ ] neutral

mothballs
- [ ] pleasant
- [ ] unpleasant
- [ ] neutral

bark mulch
- [ ] pleasant
- [ ] unpleasant
- [ ] neutral

Expose Your Nose

How to Play

This is a fun neuroscience party game for kids and adults that wakes up brain cells and stimulates memories through your sense of smell.

1. Gather small quantities of items with distinct scents, such as the following:

cedar wood	ginger
chips	chocolate
cut lemon	perfume on a cotton ball
orange peels	garlic
dirt	mothballs
mint	coffee
sawdust	onion
vanilla	pencil shavings
vinegar	

2. Place each item in a separate opaque plastic container with a lid. Do not mix the items.

3. Cut a slit in the lids large enough for players to be able to sniff, but not see, the contents.

3. Invite game players to sit in a circle.

4. Pass the first container around the circle.

5. In turn, players sniff the item in the container. (Players should only take a couple of shallow whiffs rather than inhaling deeply.)

6. After sniffing the contents of each container, players should write down:
   a. The name of the item
   b. A memory it evoked

7. Continue playing until all items have been circulated and identified, and memories captured.

8. Take turns sharing responses. Identify:
   a. Personal memories evoked by each scent
   b. Other smells that bring back strong personal memories for you

Photos Through the Decades

How to Play

Following is a photo album of events and people that made news through the decades. For each photo, attach your personal memories of the time period by responding to the five *W* questions as appropriate: who, what, where, when, why. This game can be played in a social setting with other participants. Skip any photos that represent decades that were "before your time."

Photo One: The 1950s

Who?

What?

Where?

When?

Why?

Photo Two: The 1960s

Who?

What?

Where?

When?

Why?

Photo Three: The 1970s

Who?

What?

Where?

When?

Why?

Photo Four: The 1980s

Who?

What?

Where?

When?

Why?

Photo Five: The 1990s

Who?

What?

Where?

When?

Why?

Photo Six: The 2000s

Who?

What?

Where?

When?

Why?

Memory Chargers

Here are some follow-up actions you can take to have fun while preserving and strengthening your personal episodic memories.

1. Form a social memory group (kind of like a book club) made up of family and friends. Once a month, a group member selects an event from the past and the group gets together to share personal memories and recollections. Events can be historically specific (for example, the Vietnam War), or they can be more general ("your first love," for instance, or "the best birthday you ever had"). You can enhance the experience by having the host or hostess cook a dish from that era, or by asking members to wear one piece of clothing or an accessory from that time period. Research shows that people who continue to have social connections with friends and family actively engage memory processes and live longer.

2. Create a scrapbook of important events in your life. In your scrapbook include items that will trigger cherished memories, such as photos, ticket stubs, pressed flowers, scraps of clothing, letters, e-mails, pictures cut out of travel brochures, postcards, and so on. Your creation can be a wonderful legacy piece to hand down to your children and grandchildren.

3. Make an exciting new personal memory once a month. Do something active you don't normally do. You might take a road trip, volunteer at a soup kitchen, attend a concert, go to the theater, take a walk in a national park, plan and plant a flower garden, or go out to dinner with a special someone.

4. Write your memoirs. The quality of writing doesn't matter; it's recalling the memories that counts. If you're writing in a word-processing program, download relevant photos into the text.

5. Ask one of the senior members of your family to tell you about your family's history.

   - Where and when were you born?
   - How did the family come to live there?
   - What is your earliest memory?
   - What was your favorite thing to do?
   - Did you have any pets?
   - How were holidays celebrated?
   - Where and when did you get married?

Lesson Two
Your Learning Style

Learning is like rowing upstream: not to advance is to drop back.

—Chinese Proverb

The Learning-Memory Connection

Each of us has a preferred way of learning that scientists refer to as a *learning style*. A learning style is an individual's preferred way of absorbing, processing, and acting upon new information. As we discussed in the program overview, there are three primary learning styles: visual (seeing), auditory (hearing), and experiential (doing). There is no right or wrong learning style. Your learning style is simply how you prefer to learn and take in new information. When you know your dominant learning style, you can consciously select memory techniques that complement your style.

Auditory learners can make oral and verbal connections, visual learners can use imagery and make pictoral connections, and experiential learners can make physical connections through hands-on interaction with the information to be remembered. Suppose you want to remember the name of a new mall opening in your area. It is called the Liberty Bell Mall. Visual learners might create a picture in their mind of the historic Liberty Bell located in Philadelphia. Auditory learners might repeat the name three times or ring a little hand bell three times. Experiential learners might write the name three times or draw a picture of the Liberty Bell, or do both. Neuroscientists tell us that the more connections and associations we make, the stronger our memories. Using a combination of all three learning styles creates more memory hooks by which to store and recall learned information.

Visual Learners
Visual learners find it easier to take in new information by *seeing* pictures, diagrams, charts, films, written words, and visual demonstrations. Approximately 65 percent of adults are visual learners.

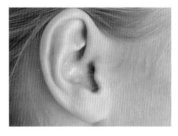

Auditory Learners
Auditory learners find it easier to take in new information by *hearing* the information spoken out loud in a lecture, on a CD or audiotape, or through oral repetition. Approximately 30 percent of adults are auditory learners.

Experiential Learners
Experiential learners find it easier to take in new information through *physical* involvement with the new information in hands-on practice opportunities. Approximately 5 percent of adults are experiential learners.

What Comes to Mind When You Think "Dog"?

The following three pictures illustrate how individuals with distinctly different learning styles make memory connections.

Visual Learner

Auditory Learner

Experiential Learner

Investigating Your Learning Style

How to Play

Take the following mini-assessment to discover your dominant learning style. In each situation, choose the numbered item that is most like you. Then check page 20.

Situation One

I just bought a new DVD player that requires assembly. In the box are parts, written directions, and a diagram. To set up the DVD player, it would be most like me to:

1. Read the directions out loud or ask someone to read them while I assemble the parts
2. Study the diagram and if necessary read the directions before assembling
3. Look at the parts, ignore the directions, and start assembling right away

Situation Two

I am interested in learning to play tennis. To explore this interest, it is most like me to

1. Talk to people who play tennis to hear what they have to say about the game
2. Find someone who plays to hit some balls to me on an actual tennis court
3. See a live match and watch an instructional video

Situation Three

My doctor told me I have to walk more to lose weight. I decide to

1. Walk on a treadmill so I can watch TV or read a magazine while I exercise
2. Get a CD player and headset so I can listen to music while I walk
3. Take up another sport; walking is too boring

Situation Four

When someone is giving a speech, I am likely to

1. Be content to sit and listen to what the speaker has to say
2. Take notes on what the speaker is presenting
3. Get restless (e.g., fiddle with my pen, tap my foot) if the speech goes on too long

Situation Five

When communicating with a friend, I enjoy

1. Exchanging e-mails, instant messaging with smiley faces, or exchanging letters
2. Stopping by spontaneously for a visit
3. Having a long and heartfelt phone conversation

Situation Six

People sometimes notice that I

1. Sing, hum, or whistle to myself
2. Doodle on my papers
3. Fidget in my seat and pick up objects and play with them

Situation Seven

When following directions for a new task, I prefer

1. Written directions
2. Seeing a demonstration of what I'm supposed to do
3. Spoken instructions

Situation Eight

When I have to teach something new to someone, I am most likely to

1. Talk them through the information
2. Write directions or diagram the information
3. Actively demonstrate what to do

Situation Nine

I am particularly good at
1. Making or repairing things with my hands
2. Anything musical
3. Visual arts

Situation Ten

When I have to go someplace new, I like to
1. Pull out a map or go to an online service that will print out written directions
2. Get in the car and figure it out as I go
3. Plug the information into the car navigator so I can hear the directions spoken out loud

Situation Eleven

When I am trying to drive home a point, I am likely to use phrases such as
1. "Can you see it?," "Can you imagine it?," and "Can you picture it?"
2. "Can you sense it?" and "Can you feel it?"
3. "Does it sound right?" and "Does it ring a bell?"

Situation Twelve

When I read, I particularly notice
1. Action scenes
2. How the words flow and fit together like poetry
3. Descriptive scenes in which I imagine myself as the hero or heroine

Situation Thirteen

When I am trying to concentrate, I become distracted by
1. People moving around, or general untidiness
2. Sounds, noises, or people talking out loud
3. People engaging in a physical activity nearby

Situation Fourteen

If I am trying to spell an unfamiliar word, I am most likely to
1. Write the word down, playing with it until it feels right
2. Sound the word out phonetically
3. Try to picture the word in my mind

Situation Fifteen

When meeting a casual acquaintance for the second time, I am most likely to recall
1. Where we met
2. What we did together
3. What we talked about

Situation Sixteen

When I am conversing with someone, I
1. Enjoy listening but am eager to jump in and speak
2. Speak sparingly and watch the other person's facial expressions as he or she talks
3. Gesture and use expressive movements when talking

Situation Seventeen

When relaxing, I prefer to
1. Watch a film or video, go to the theater, or read a book
2. Listen to music or attend a lecture or concert
3. Play games, play sports, or make things with my hands

Situation Eighteen

To let someone know he or she did a good job, I am likely to
1. Give the person a pat on the back
2. Praise the individual orally
3. Write the individual an e-mail, a note, or a card

Your Learning Style—Answers

Here is the answer key for the preceding learning style self-assessment. As you review your responses, put a check mark next to your response for each situation. Then count up the number of check marks for each learning style (i.e., visual, auditory, experiential). The learning style with the highest number of check marks represents your primary learning style.

Situation One
1. Auditory
2. Visual
3. Experiential

Situation Two
1. Auditory
2. Experiential
3. Visual

Situation Three
1. Visual
2. Auditory
3. Experiential

Situation Four
1. Auditory
2. Visual
3. Experiential

Situation Five
1. Visual
2. Experiential
3. Auditory

Situation Six
1. Auditory
2. Visual
3. Experiential

Situation Seven
1. Visual
2. Experiential
3. Auditory

Situation Eight
1. Auditory
2. Visual
3. Experiential

Situation Nine
1. Experiential
2. Auditory
3. Visual

Situation Ten
1. Visual
2. Experiential
3. Auditory

Situation Eleven
1. Visual
2. Experiential
3. Auditory

Situation Twelve
1. Experiential
2. Auditory
3. Visual

Situation Thirteen
1. Visual
2. Auditory
3. Experiential

Situation Fourteen
1. Experiential
2. Auditory
3. Visual

Situation Fifteen
1. Visual
2. Experiential
3. Auditory

Situation Sixteen
1. Auditory
2. Visual
3. Experiential

Situation Seventeen
1. Visual
2. Auditory
3. Experiential

Situation Eighteen
1. Experiential
2. Auditory
3. Visual

Making the Most of Your Learning Style

Now that you've discovered your dominant learning style, here is a personalized tip sheet to help you make the most of your learning style when faced with remembering important information at home, school, or work.

Visual Learners

- Write down key facts in an outline or other visual representation that connects the ideas.
- Visualize what you are learning through vivid mental pictures.
- Create pictures and diagrams of what you are learning.
- Use visual timelines for remembering dates.
- Make up strong visual image links.
- Use pictures, charts, film, video, graphics, and so forth.
- Take notes, underline, and highlight.

Auditory Learners

- Listen to a seminar, presentation, or explanation.
- Read aloud to yourself.
- Read with emotion or an accent.
- Make a tape of key points to listen to in the car or while doing chores.
- Verbally summarize key points in your own words.
- Explain the subject to someone else.
- Have someone quiz you out loud.
- Use your own internal voice to verbalize what you are learning.

Experiential Learners

- Copy a demonstration.
- Create flash cards that capture key points.
- Record information as you hear it in an action flowchart, using arrows and other dynamic symbols.
- Walk around while you read.
- Underline and highlight key points and new information.
- Put key points on index cards and sort them into an order, such as alphabetical or chronological.
- Learn by doing.

Visual Learner

Auditory Learner

Experiential Learner

Memory Chargers

Here are some follow-up actions you can take to strengthen your memory through the use of the three learning styles.

1. Practice experiencing the world around you through each of the three learning styles. When you go for a walk or are driving, focus on each learning style one at a time for five minutes; then switch to another style. Here's how it works:

   Visual: Look for five colorful images you never noticed before along your walking or driving route. When you get home, write down from memory the five new images you noticed and how they made you feel.

   Auditory: Listen for five varied sounds that catch your attention (such as a bird singing, an ambulance siren, etc.). When you get home, write down from memory the five things you heard and how they made you feel.

   Experiential: Notice five unusual or exciting actions that are occurring as you walk or drive along. When you get home, write down from memory the actions you noticed and how they made you feel.

2. Engage in a new learning activity that requires you to draw on the strengths of a learning style that is not your preferred style. For instance:

   Visual Learners: Take a step aerobics class or learn a new style of dancing that requires you to jump into the action and learn as you go.

   Auditory Learners: Watch an old silent film. After viewing the film, re-create the plot through a simple stick-figure drawing.

   Experiential Learners: Learn how to play a new sport or build something by watching a how-to video or reading a how-to book.

3. Identify a few memory snafus that drive you nuts, such as forgetting where you parked your car or not remembering the name of a movie you just saw. Make a conscious effort to remember this information using your preferred learning style. For instance, suppose you want to remember the name of the hit comedy movie *In Her Shoes*. Here are some ways you might remember by using your preferred learning style:

   Visual Learners: Imagine yourself, or your significant other, stepping into lipstick-red satin shoes, with sparkly straps that go halfway up the calf.

   Auditory Learners: Make up a rhyme that fits the story line—"The girl who stepped into her sister's shoes ended up with a case of the blues."

   Experiential Learners: Tap your heels together three times.

4. For additional practice, try creating a memory connection for each of the following items, using each of the dominant learning styles.

   pick up bread • remember friend's birthday • get dog food • return library book • make airline reservation • pick up flowers for anniversary • return phone call

Working Memories Made Easy

The brain is a world consisting of a number of unexplored continents and great stretches of unknown territory.

—Santiago Ramón y Cajal, 1906 Nobel Prize winner (with Camillo Golgi) for work on the structure of the nervous system

How Are Memories Made?

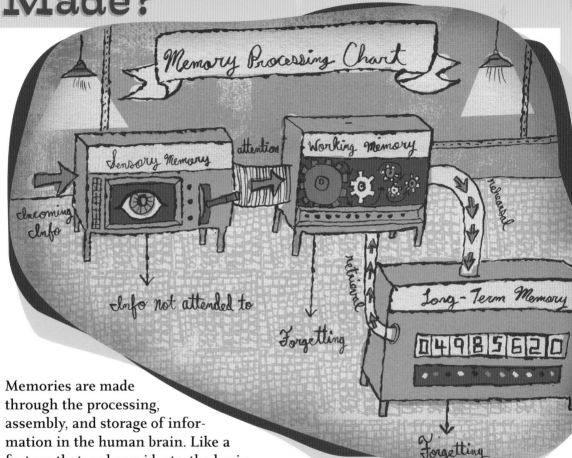

Memories are made through the processing, assembly, and storage of information in the human brain. Like a factory that makes widgets, the brain starts with raw material and converts it into a final memory product, which, if all goes well, is stored in the long-term memory to be recalled later when needed. Just like in a factory, however, sometimes the process breaks down. When this happens, memories can be faulty or lost.

Sensory Stimuli

The raw material of memories is the *sensory stimuli* that we receive through our five senses: sight, sound, touch, smell, and taste, certain of which are directly linked to our preferred learning style. Experts theorize that visual learners pay more attention to the sense of sight than to the other senses, auditory learners pay more attention to the sense of sound, and experiential learners pay more attention to the sense of touch.

Sensory information enters the brain whether or not we are paying attention. For example, these words are producing visual sensory stimuli, whether or not you are really concentrating. Other senses are also entering the memory factory in a preconscious way. For example, in your peripheral vision you may glimpse your coffee mug. If your window is open, you may hear children playing outside, a dog barking, or an ambulance whizzing along. The impression of random *sensory input* on the brain is the first phase in the production of a memory.

Working Memory

The second phase in making a memory is called *selective attention*. In this phase, we consciously choose to pay attention to certain sensory stimuli. When the operator recites an important number we wish to remember, we consciously pay attention to the sound of the numbers being spoken. If we see and hear that an ambulance is stopping in front of our house, these sensory perceptions rise to our consciousness and take on meaning, while other, irrelevant stimuli fade out and are lost. Sensory stimuli that we choose to pay attention to are temporarily stored in our *working memory*. Working memory is the brain's scratch pad for capturing information needed to accomplish an immediate goal or task. For example, when comparing the prices of two similar items in the grocery store, we focus on the dollar amounts and quantities just long enough to make a purchasing decision.

Long-term Memory

The third phase of memory production is the conversion of select *working memories* into *long-term memories*. Converting a working memory into a long-term memory requires some form of elaborate rehearsal. If you want to remember your friend's phone number without looking it up, you will need to make a conscious effort to memorize the number through one of a series of reinforcement techniques.

Recall and Recognition

We *retrieve* memories from long-term memory by recalling the information or by recognizing the information. *Recall* is the memory function of calling up learned information and past experiences on demand. An example of this function would be recalling without a prompt the date Columbus arrived in the New World. *Recognition* is the memory function of remembering information when we see it. An example of this would be choosing the correct response from a multiple-choice question. We can boost our brain's own memory processes by consciously choosing to use our learning style to help us make a stronger memory connection. Think of how you learned the alphabet in school by using a melody. This is an example of auditory learning. Visual learners have been known to remember the key points in a speech by visualizing each point as an image sitting on a different body part, with the first point located on their head and the last point located on their feet.

In this lesson, you'll learn more about the critical processes of working memory and long-term memory. You'll also get the chance to experiment with your preferred learning style as you engage in compelling games designed to stimulate your working memory and your long-term memory. We'll begin with working memory.

Your Memory's Scratch Pad

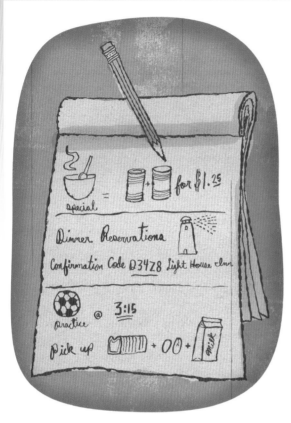

Working memory, frequently called *short-term memory*, is your memory's scratch pad. It is a place where information that might get committed to long-term memory is temporarily stored. Working memories last from a few seconds to as long as about a minute. The storage capacity for working memory is quite small, holding only three to seven pieces of information for the few seconds it takes to execute a current task, such as jotting down a new phone number, keeping your place in a conversation, or adding up the price of groceries in your grocery basket.

Working memory has its soft spots. People may be able to memorize an infinite number of facts, but only a small number of items can be held and accessed in working memory. This explains why we can recall a fact learned many years ago in school but easily forget an item or two on our grocery list. In addition to being able to hold only a very limited amount of information, working memory is also very vulnerable to distractions. Have you ever lost your train of thought in a conversation, or gone into a room and forgotten why you were there? This happens when an interruption causes you to momentarily lose focus, short-circuiting your working memory. As we age, we become more susceptible to distractions and interruptions, and the storage capacity of our working memory diminishes somewhat.

You can improve your working memory at any age. By exercising your working memory, you can strengthen and build memory muscle in the same way that physical exercise builds muscle strength. You are about to enter the working-memory gym, where you'll play a series of fun and engaging memory games designed to recharge your working memory.

Number Span

How to Play

Typically people can hold no more than three to seven items of information in working memory. To determine the storage capacity of your working memory, read each set of numbers at right out loud, one set at a time. After you have read a set, look away, and try to recall the numbers in the set in the order presented. Continue working your way down the number sets until your working memory short-circuits. You might find it more comfortable to block out the sets you've already read with a piece of paper. The last set of numbers you can accurately recall is one measure of the storage capacity of your working memory for numbers.

Number Span

879

3064

71285

537249

4072396

90234816

639718420

8032975814

Memory Assessment

Needs improvement: Recalled 1-2 numbers

Average: Recalled 3-4 numbers

Good: Recalled 5-6 numbers

Very good: Recalled 7-8 numbers

Excellent: Recalled 9-10 numbers

Memory Booster

Chunking numbers into smaller groups will boost your ability to store and recall numbers. For example, if the number is 8653, then chunk this large number into two smaller numbers: 86 and 53. Also look for familiar *associations* among the numbers in a set. The number 86, for instance, might be the age of your grandmother or the exit you take on the highway to get home. Auditory learners might try singing the number chunks (any random melody will do). Visual and experiential learners might try tracing the numbers.

Word Span

Word Span

banana, clock, box

bell, apple, table, glass

chair, airplane, camera, hammer, beetle

spoon, telephone, lamp, house, scissors, car

tree, guitar, ball, corn, flower, bird's nest, sofa

cow, bike, bee, shoe, eye, book, glass, fork

book, basket, tree, pencil, star, moon, ring, heart, knife

stairs, bandage, hand, nurse, hospital, ambulance, stretcher, chart, pen, blood

How to Play

Here is a variation of the number-span game using common words instead of numbers. Recite each word in a set out loud, proceeding down the sets one at a time. After you have recited the words in one set, look away, and try to recall the words in that set in the order presented. Continue working your way down the word sets until your working memory short-circuits. You might find it helpful to block out the sets you've already read with a piece of paper. The last set of words you can accurately recall is one measure of the storage capacity of your working memory for words.

Memory Assessment

Needs improvement: Recalled 1-2 words

Average: Recalled 3-4 words

Good: Recalled 5-6 words

Very food: Recalled 7-8 words

Excellent: Recalled 9-10 words

Memory Booster

Linking two or more words in a set will boost your working memory capacity. There are different ways to link words. Using a visual learning style, you might link the images the words represent in a picture. Drawing on an experiential and visual learning style, you might connect the word images in an action story. Let's say the words to be remembered are *kite*, *dog*, and *scissors*. You might visualize a dog chasing a kite, or a hole in the kite made by a pair of snapping scissors. Auditory learners might want to repeat the words out loud three times.

Scattered Objects

How to Play

Study the objects in the box for 45 seconds. Then cover the box and write down the names of all the objects you can remember. The number of objects you can remember is one measure of your working memory's storage capacity

  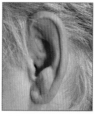 

 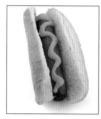  

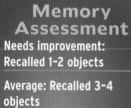   

for visual images.

Memory Assessment

Needs improvement: Recalled 1-2 objects

Average: Recalled 3-4 objects

Good: Recalled 5-6 objects

Very good: Recalled 7-8 objects

Excellent: Recalled 9-10 objects

Memory Booster

To give your working memory a boost, look for humorous and dynamic ways to *link* two or more objects. Using a visual learning style, you might picture the toothbrush inside the hot dog bun with mustard instead of toothpaste on the brush. Using an experiential learning style, you might create action scenes with humorous or emotional punch. For instance, you might imagine the rabbit eating the ice cream cone. Using an auditory learning style, you might connect words that begin with the same letter sound, repeating them out loud with a special vocal punch on the common letter sound (e.g., bun, bowl, brush).

Colorful Stories

How to Play

In this game, you will be presented with a series of sentences. The sentences are related and form a little story. In each sentence the color of an object will be mentioned. Read each sentence and try to memorize the "color" words (e.g., red, blue) mentioned in each one. Below each story, you will be asked to recall the color words. You will also be thrown an *interference* curveball. Prior to recalling the colors, you will be asked to answer a simple question related to the story. Despite this "distraction," your challenge is to keep the colors in your working memory.

Memory Booster

Look for ways to lock color patterns in your memory. For instance, imagine a rainbow made up of the colors in the story. Or try sorting the colors into categories such as bold and dull, or light and dark. Using a visual learning style, you might try linking the color to its visual image (for example: brown bear, ebony piano, red door, indigo sky). Using an experiential learning style, you might create dynamic interactions among the color images (such as a brown bear playing a tune on the ebony piano). Using an auditory learning style, you might try linking the first letters of the colors to form wordlike sounds that will serve as memory prompts (e.g., brown, ebony, red, indigo = beri)

Story One

Read the following sentences carefully and try to memorize the colors mentioned. Then cover the sentences and answer the questions below. (Answers are on page 143.)

The child sat pensively looking out the window at the gray, falling rain while her mother played a Bach concerto on the ebony grand piano.

Suddenly, there was a loud knock on the door announcing that the golden carriage of the king had arrived.

The excitement in the small red farmhouse rose as everyone's thoughts turned to the ball.

The old brown spaniel lifted his head and barked dutifully, announcing the entry of the king's entourage.

1. What composer is mentioned?
- ☐ Bach
- ☐ Beethoven
- ☐ Brahms

2. What colors are mentioned?
1. _____
2. _____
3. _____
4. _____
5. _____

Memory Assessment

Needs improvement: Recalled 1-2 colors

Average: Recalled 3 colors

Good: Recalled 4 colors

Excellent: Recalled 5 colors

Story Two

Read the following sentences carefully and try to memorize the colors mentioned. Then cover the sentences and answer the questions below. (Answers are on page 143.)

The black bear wandered out of the green forest in search of food after a long and snowy winter.

She picked up the scent of red meat cooking on a barbecue in a nearby campground.

The campers, unaware of the bear, were washing their clothes in the crystal blue stream.

The bear rose on her hind legs and let out a roar as she approached, proceeding to eat the meat along with a pot of brown beans.

1. What were the campers doing when the bear arrived?
   ☐ Eating barbecue
   ☐ Swimming in the river
   ☐ Washing laundry

2. What colors are mentioned?
   1. _____
   2. _____
   3. _____
   4. _____
   5. _____

Memory Assessment

Needs improvement: Recalled 1-2 colors

Average: Recalled 3 colors

Good: Recalled 4 colors

Excellent: Recalled 5 colors

Story Three

Read the following sentences carefully and try to memorize the colors mentioned. Then cover the sentences and answer the questions below. (Answers are on page 143.)

The woman arrived on Air France from Paris with her white toy poodle under her arm.

She was met by Officer Ouelette, the chief of police, who escorted her through a blue door into the holding room.

She nervously tapped her long pink fingernails on the glass tabletop.

Officer Ouelette turned his attention to the gray file on his desk.

Picking up his red pen, he began to write on a clean sheet of white paper.

1. What airline did the woman arrive on?
- [ ] British Airways
- [ ] Air Italia
- [ ] Air France

2. What colors are mentioned?
1. _____
2. _____
3. _____
4. _____
5. _____

Memory Assessment

Needs improvement: Recalled 1-2 colors

Average: Recalled 3 colors

Good: Recalled 4 colors

Excellent: Recalled 5 colors

Story Four

Read the following sentences carefully and try to memorize the colors mentioned. Then cover the sentences and answer the questions below. (Answers are on page 143.)

The Lake Morey Resort is located in Fairlee, Vermont, in the heart of the Green Mountains.

During the winter the major attraction is downhill skiing, but when the white snow melts and the weather turns warm, the skiers are replaced by golfers who come to play on the lush green fairways that are home to the Vermont Open.

Summer in Vermont is picture perfect, with sparkling blue lakes surrounded by towering green mountains that beckon swimmers and boaters alike.

At Lake Morey, one is often treated to the sight of brightly colored hot air balloons floating lazily in a cloudless, azure sky.

Families are welcome and children will find a traditional playground with sturdy swings, slides, and climbing bars held securely in place by gray metal poles cemented into the ground.

1. Where is the Lake Morey Resort located?
   - ☐ Fairlee, Vermont
   - ☐ Morey, Vermont
   - ☐ White Mountain, Vermont

2. What colors are mentioned?
   1. _____
   2. _____
   3. _____
   4. _____
   5. _____

Memory Assessment

Needs improvement; Recalled 1–2 colors

Average: Recalled 3 colors

Good: Recalled 4 colors

Excellent: Recalled 5 colors

Story Five

Read the following sentences carefully and try to memorize the colors mentioned. Then cover the sentences and answer the questions below. (Answers are on page 143.)

The old Victorian house was dark, with the exception of a tiny pinpoint of yellow light coming from a window on the upper level.

Approaching the house at night was a bit unnerving, with only a flashlight and a sliver of a silver moon to guide the way.

Upon approaching the structure, I was surprised to see that it had been freshly painted in soft rose hues reminiscent of a child's dollhouse.

I lifted the large brass knocker on the old mahogany door and rapped three times in quick succession.

I was greeted by an Irish lass with keen green eyes that warned of danger.

With a toss of her auburn hair, she bid me enter through a china blue doorway.

1. What was the style of the house?
   ☐ Victorian
   ☐ English Tudor
   ☐ Contemporary

2. What colors are mentioned?
   1. _____
   2. _____
   3. _____
   4. _____
   5. _____
   6. _____
   7. _____

Memory Assessment

Needs improvement: Recalled 1-2 colors

Average: Recalled 3-4 colors

Good: Recalled 5 colors

Very good: Recalled 6 colors

Excellent: Recalled 7 colors

Story Six

Read the following sentences carefully and try to memorize the colors mentioned. Then cover the sentences and answer the questions below. (Answers are on page 143.)

The schoolchildren, ranging in age from seven to thirteen, entered the great hall dressed smartly in their blue uniforms.

Behind the podium was the grand wizard himself, standing regally erect in his purple, ceremonial robes.

The children settled themselves into the rows of gray benches adorned with velvety red cushions.

The grand wizard knocked on the podium with a large brown gavel, and a hush fell over the hall.

"I've come to talk to you about a great danger lurking on our peaceful grounds," said the wizard. It is the black wolf we call "Sevy," who can transform himself at will into many evil manifestations.

"Do not look directly into his golden eyes, for they will blind you to the truth of his evil intentions," warned the wizard.

1. On what were the children sitting?
   ☐ Chairs
   ☐ Benches
   ☐ Stools

2. What colors are mentioned?
   1. _____
   2. _____
   3. _____
   4. _____
   5. _____
   6. _____
   7. _____

Memory Assessment

Needs improvement: Recalled 1-2 colors

Average: Recalled 3-4 colors

Good: Recalled 5 colors

Very good: Recalled 6 colors

Excellent: Recalled 7 colors

Story Seven

Read the following sentences carefully and try to memorize the colors mentioned. Then cover the sentences and answer the questions below. (Answers are on page 143.)

At Shannon Airport, we rented an older-model red Citroën with an automatic shift to take us on a journey through western Ireland.

We started out in County Clare, where our first stop as tourists was the rugged Cliffs of Moher, with their spectacular view of the Aran Islands and the foaming green Atlantic Ocean.

Our next destination was the Dingle Peninsula in County Kerry, where our first vivid impression was of the colorful fishing boats in various hues of orange and blue.

After a pleasant stay in Dingle Bay, where we did some shopping and shared a pint of dark brown Guinness beer in a local pub, we traveled on to Killarney National Park. Here we wandered through the colorful and orderly gardens of the Muckross Estate, later taking a horse-and-buggy ride across the grounds to Ross Castle. Our buggy came complete with red plaid blankets against the cold and a charming Irishman dressed in traditional green who filled us in on the history of the castle.

One of my favorite adventures of all was the two-hundred-yard descent in near blackness into the ancient Doolin Cave, where we came upon a gleaming white stalactite, the longest in the Northern Hemisphere, measuring approximately twenty feet long.

1. In which county did the tourists begin their travels through Ireland?
   - ☐ County Galway
   - ☐ County Kerry
   - ☐ County Clare

2. What colors are mentioned?
   1. _____
   2. _____
   3. _____
   4. _____
   5. _____
   6. _____
   7. _____

Memory Assessment

Needs improvement: Recalled 1–2 colors

Average: Recalled 3–4 colors

Good: Recalled 5 colors

Very good: Recalled 6 colors

Excellent: Recalled 7 colors

Xs and Os

How to Play

Take 30 seconds to memorize the location of the *X*s and *O*s in each box of the table. Then cover the table and wait 30 seconds. Look at the empty table below and write the *X*s and *O*s in the shaded boxes exactly where you saw them. As you progress, the shading cues will be reduced, which will increase the difficulty of the challenge.

Set One

X		X
	X	
	O	
O		

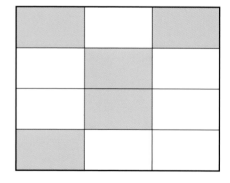

Memory Assessment

Needs improvement: Placed 1-2 symbols correctly

Average: Placed 3 symbols correctly

Good: Placed 4 symbols correctly

Excellent: Placed 5 symbols correctly

Set Two

Memorize the physical location of the *X* and *O* symbols in each box of the table. Allow yourself 30 seconds, and then go on to the empty table on the next page.

	X		**O**
		O	
X			
	O		**X**

Memory Booster

If you're an experiential learner, try using your forefinger to "tap in" the location of the Xs and Os. Auditory learners who are musical might "sing" the symbol locations as if they were notes on a musical scale. Visual learners will want to look for optical patterns and spatial relationships.

Insert the *X* and *O* symbols in the correct shaded and unshaded boxes to match their physical location above. There are six symbols in total.

Memory Assessment

Needs improvement: Placed 1-2 symbols correctly

Average: Placed 3 symbols correctly

Good: Placed 4 symbols correctly

Very good: Placed 5 symbols correctly

Excellent: Placed 6 symbols correctly

Set Three

Memorize the physical location of the X and O symbols in each box of the table. Allow yourself 45 seconds, and then go on to the empty table on the next page.

			X	
	X			X
O		O		
		X		O

Insert the X and O symbols in the correct shaded and unshaded boxes to match their physical location above. There are seven symbols in total.

Originals and Imposters

Memory Skills:
Recall

Memory Process:
Working Memory

Challenge Level:

How to Play

You will be presented with a set of original images. Study the images in the original set for 30 seconds. Then turn the page and try to find the original images among the imposters.

Set One

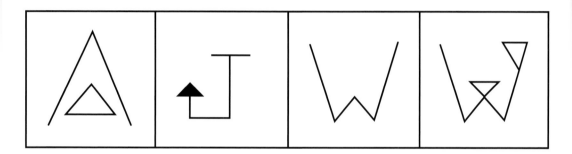

Memory Booster

Look for one or more distinguishing characteristics of each abstract image to lock it in your memory. Does the image, or a part of the image, bear a resemblance to a familiar object? Is there a spatial orientation that would help you differentiate the original from an imposter? Does the image, or a part of the image, face north, south, east, or west?

Place an *X* under each image you recognize from the original set.

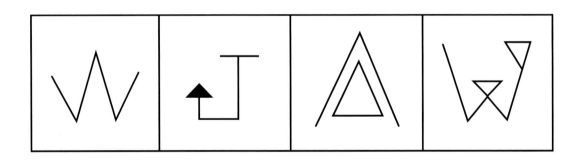

Set Two

Study the images in the original set below. Then look at the next page and locate the original images among the imposters. Place an *X* under each figure you recognize.

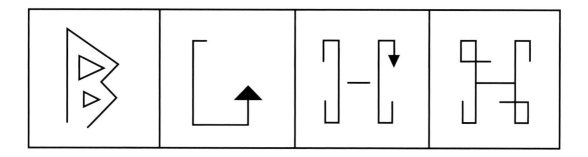

Place an X under each image you recognize from the original set.

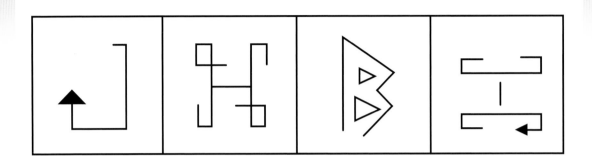

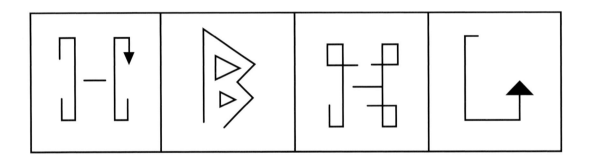

Set Three

Study the images in the original set below. Then look at the next page and locate the original images among the imposters. Place an *X* under each original image you recognize.

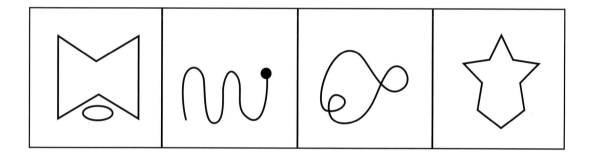

Place an X under each figure you recognize from the original set.

Set Four

Study the images in the original set. Then look at the next page and locate the original images among the imposters. Place an X under each original image you recognize.

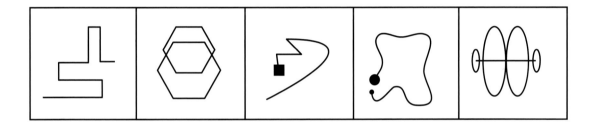

Place an *X* under each image you recognize from the original set.

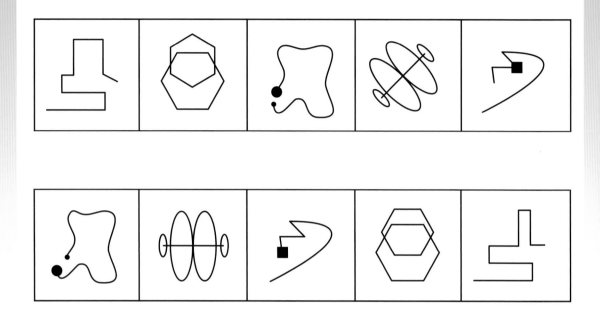

Zodiac Signs

How to Play

You will be presented with the graphic symbols of the zodiac signs for each season of the year: winter, spring, summer, and autumn. Each season has three zodiac symbols. Your challenge is to study the zodiac symbols and then draw them from memory. You can create your own level of challenge by taking on one symbol at a time, two symbols at a time, or all three at once.

Memory Booster

To give your memory a boost, try to associate each symbol with a familiar shape or object. For instance, the zodiac symbol for Leo looks a little like a horseshoe. Visual learners might conjure up the image of a lion with a horseshoe around its neck. Experiential learners might try tracing over the lines lightly with the tip of a pencil. Auditory learners could try speaking the name of the sign and its image out loud (e.g., "Leo, horse, shoe").

Study each season for one minute, then
cover the row and reproduce the seasonal
zodiac symbols

Winter Zodiac Symbols

December 23–January 20	January 21–February 19	February 20–March 20
Capricorn	Aquarius	Pisces

Spring Zodiac Symbols

March 21–April 20	April 21–May 21	May 22–June 21
Aries	Taurus	Gemini

Summer Zodiac Symbols

June 22–July 23	July 24–August 23	August 24–September 23
Cancer	Leo	Virgo

Autumn Zodiac Symbol

September 24–October 23	October 24–November 22	November 23–December 22
Libra	Scorpio	Sagittarius

Block Patterns

How to Play

Study the pattern of the letters and numbers in each block, one block at a time, for 30 seconds. Then cover each block and reproduce it on a separate piece of scrap paper, placing the numbers and letters in the exact same formation as the original.

Block Pattern One

O P 1

W R 2

L A 3

Block Pattern Two

B 7 I

A G S

5 8 3

Memory Booster

To boost your memory, look for familiar associations among the numbers and letters. Do you see a word hidden in the formation? What numbers or letters create a vertical or horizontal line? Do the number or letter arrangements form a familiar shape? Which letters or numbers are in color? Experiential learners should trace the familiar words and patterns with their fingers. Visual learners should determine the spatial orientation (i.e., horizontal, vertical, diagonal) of the familiar words and patterns. Auditory learners should repeat the familiar words and shapes out loud three times, moving from one spatial orientation to another.

Block Pattern Three

9 O 3

J 7 H

6 N X

Block Pattern Four

5 U M

L 8 E

P B 6

Block Pattern Five

M V 8

O A E

6 T D

Memory Assessment

Needs improvement: Reproduced less than one third of each formation

Good: Reproduced one third of each formation

Very good: Reproduced two thirds of each formation

Excellent: Reproduced all of each formation

Memory Chargers

Here are some follow-up games you can play alone or with friends and family to exercise your working memory.

Game One: Now You See It, Now You Don't

1. Have a partner place ten to twenty objects on a tray; then cover the objects with a cloth. Remove the cloth, and view the objects for one minute. Cover the objects with the cloth and write down the names of all the objects you can remember.

2. Have a partner place ten to twelve objects on a tray in a specific spatial arrangement; then cover the objects with a cloth. Remove the cloth, and view the objects and their locations for one minute. Cover the tray and shake the tray to redistribute the objects. Remove the cloth and try to place the objects back in their original locations.

Game Two: Let's Face It

1. Have a partner cut ten to twelve faces of famous and familiar people out of a magazine. Place the cutout faces on a tray, and then cover them with a cloth. Remove the cloth and study the faces for one minute. Cover the faces and try to write down the names of all the people you saw.

2. Have a partner cut ten to twelve faces of random people out of a magazine and place them on a tray in a specific spatial arrange-

ment; then cover the tray. (Vary the faces to include gender and ethnic diversity.) Remove the cloth and study the faces and their locations for one minute. Cover the faces with a cloth and shake the tray to redistribute the faces. Remove the cloth and try to place the faces back in their original locations.

Game Three: Concentration

Using a deck of playing cards, pull out fifteen matched pairs (a total of thirty cards). Mix up the cards, and then arrange them facedown in a six-by-five grid. One player turns over two cards at a time (take a look at the next page). If the overturned cards match, the player picks up the two cards, sets them aside, and turns over two more cards. If the two cards do not match, the player returns them facedown to their original positions, and it is the next player's turn. The winner of the game is the one who has acquired the most matches. To increase the challenge level, use the whole deck of cards (twenty-six matched pairs). The object of the game is to remember where matching cards are located and to pick up as many matching pairs as possible. (Try playing the concentration game online at www.brainfit.net.)

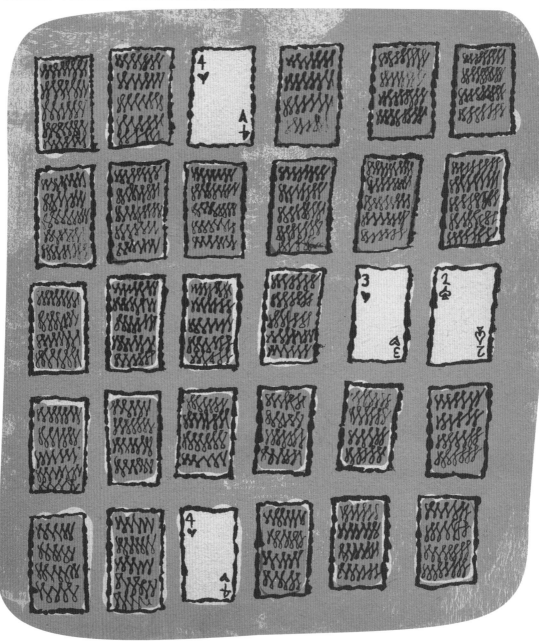

Long-term Memories That Last

Humans are born time travelers. We may not be able to send our bodies into the past or the future, at least not yet, but we can send our minds. We can relive events that happened long ago or envision ourselves in the future.

—Carl Zimmer, "Time in the Animal Mind," *New York Times*, April 3, 2007

Your Memory's Storage Bins

Long-term memory is the phase of the memory process considered the permanent storehouse of information. Long-term memories are stored as "meaning" and can last for a lifetime. Unlike working memory, long-term memory experiences little decay over time, and we can mentally travel back in time to retrieve and revisit these memories. There are two types of long-term memory: episodic memory and semantic memory. You worked with episodic memory in Lesson One. Episodic memory captures events we have personally experienced. *Semantic memory* captures facts, concepts, and skills we have acquired through repetitive exposure and rote learning.

Memory Storage

Two main activities are related to long-term memory: storage and retrieval. Information in working memory is transferred and stored in long-term memory by rehearsal and repetition. Most researchers agree that new information must be rehearsed a minimum of three times to secure the information in long-term memory. Suppose you want to remember the name of a new acquaintance. Here is a simple rehearsal strategy for remembering a new name that applies the "rule of three" and draws on learning styles. First, visualize yourself writing the name using a red marker, one capital letter at a time, on your mind's blackboard (visual learning style). (Experiential learners might want to trace the name on their palm.) Next, use the name in conversation three times (auditory learning style). Finally, look for a memory hook by which to create meaning. For example, if the new name is Henry, create a meaningful memory hook by linking the name Henry to the infamous Henry VIII, who had six wives, two of whom he beheaded, two of whom he divorced, and one of whom he humiliatingly rejected. Picture your Henry with a crown on his head, made of six linked golden wedding bands. (You'll learn more about creating meaningful memory hooks in Lesson Six, "Make an Association.")

Memory Retrieval

Retrieval is the process of calling up information stored in long-term memory through the mental activities of recall and recognition. In recall, the information is reproduced from memory in response to a thought or question. In recognition, it is the presentation of the information itself that prompts knowledge that the information is familiar and has been seen before. Recognition is a far less complex activity than recall.

Long-Term Memory

In this lesson, you'll engage in a series of games that prompt your brain to retrieve facts and general knowledge stored in your long-term memory through the activities of recall and recognition. Information that was learned well through repeated exposure, rehearsal, and meaningful associations will be easier to remember than information learned in a cursory way.

Classic TV Jingles

How to Play

You will be presented with a series of well-known television commercial jingles. Your challenge is to name the product or brand that goes with the jingle.

1. Snap! Crackle! Pop!: _____
2. Put a tiger in your tank: _____
3. Sometimes you feel like a nut, sometimes you don't: _____
4. Breakfast of champions: _____
5. If you've got the time, we've got the beer: _____
6. Because I'm worth it: _____
7. The most trusted name in news: _____
8. The best part of waking up: _____
9. I'm a pepper, he's a pepper, she's a pepper: _____
10. Tony the Tiger says, "They're grrrrreat!": _____
11. Double your pleasure, double your fun: _____
12. The real mayonnaise: _____
13. Everyone doesn't like something, but nobody doesn't like: _____
14. M'm! M'm! Good!: _____
15. From the valley of the Jolly (ho, ho, ho): _____
16. When you care enough to send the very best: _____
17. Sorry, Charlie: _____
18. Plop, plop, fizz, fizz: _____
19. It's not nice to fool Mother Nature: _____
20. We do chicken right: _____
21. You deserve a break today: _____
22. Must see TV: _____
23. It's the real thing: _____
24. What's in your wallet?: _____
25. See the USA in your: _____
26. Fly the friendly skies of: _____
27. Be all that you can be: _____
28. Can you hear me now?: _____
29. We do it your way: _____
30. A little dab'll do ya: _____

Memory Assessment

Needs improvement: Gave 1-7 correct responses

Average: Gave 8-10 correct responses

Good: Gave 11-17 correct responses

Very good: Gave 18-25 correct responses

Excellent: Gave 25-30 correct responses

Memory Booster

Draw on a visual learning style by trying to see the product or brand logo in your mind's eye. Draw on an auditory learning style by singing the jingle or saying out loud the words associated with the jingle. Draw on an experiential learning style by re-creating in your mind the actions associated with the jingle's television commercial.

Movie Mania

How to Play

You will be presented with well-known quotes spoken by famous actors in classic movies. Your long-term memory challenge is to name the movies in which the lines were spoken.

Quote	Actor	Movie
1. "Frankly, my dear, I don't give a damn."	Clark Gable	_____
2. "I'm going to make him an offer he can't refuse."	Marlon Brando	_____
3. "Snap out of it!"	Cher	_____
4. "Toto, I've got a feeling we're not in Kansas anymore."	Judy Garland	_____
5. "Here's looking at you, kid."	Humphrey Bogart	_____
6. "Go ahead, make my day."	Clint Eastwood	_____
7. "May the Force be with you."	Harrison Ford	_____
8. "We rob banks."	Warren Beatty	_____
9. "You had me at hello."	Renée Zellweger	_____
10. "I love the smell of napalm in the morning."	Robert Duvall	_____
11. "E.T. phone home."	Pat Welsh	_____
12. "A census taker once tried to test me. I ate his liver with some fava beans and a nice Chianti."	Anthony Hopkins	_____
13. "We're gonna need a bigger boat."	Roy Scheider	_____

Memory Booster

If you can't immediately retrieve the name of the movie, try recalling other facts associated with the movie to prompt your memory, including:

Where, when, and with whom you saw the movie.

The plot of the movie.

The names of other actors in the movie.

Some other famous lines from the movie.

A dramatic scene from the movie in which the actor listed is present.

14. "There's no place like home."   Judy Garland   _____

15. "Show me the money!"   Cuba Gooding   _____

16. "After all, tomorrow is another day!"   Vivien Leigh   _____

17. "I'll have what she's having."   Estelle Reiner   _____

18. "I'm the king of the world."   Leonardo DiCaprio   _____

19. "If you build it, he will come."   Kevin Costner   _____

20. "Mama always said life was like a box of chocolates.
    You never know what you're gonna get."   Tom Hanks   _____

21. "Houston, we have a problem."   Tom Hanks   _____

22. "Mrs. Robinson, you're trying to seduce me. Aren't you?"   Dustin Hoffman   _____

23. "Of all the gin joints in all the towns in all the world,
    she walks into mine."   Humphrey Bogart   _____

24. "Hasta la vista, baby."   Arnold
                                                                  Schwarzenegger   _____

25. "Carpe diem. Seize the day, boys. Make your lives
    extraordinary."   Robin Williams   _____

26. "Nobody puts Baby in a corner."   Patrick Swayze   _____

27. "Welcome to the Caribbean, love."   Johnny Depp   _____

28. "Tell 'em to go out there with all they got and win just
    one for the Gipper."   Ronald Reagan   _____

29. "Yo, Adrian!"   Sylvester Stallone   _____

30. "I see dead people."   Haley Joel Osment   _____

Memory Assessment

Needs improvement: Gave 1-9 correct responses

Average: Gave 10-14 correct responses

Good: Gave 15-19 correct responses

Very good: Gave 20-29 correct responses

Excellent: Gave 30 correct responses

Words of Wisdom

How to Play

You will be presented with a series of proverbs. Your long-term memory challenge is to complete the last word of each proverb. Playing with a friend? Split the list and see who can fill in the blanks first.

1. A bird in the hand is worth two in the _____.

2. A chain is no stronger than its weakest _____.

3. A person is known by the company he/she _____.

4. A rolling stone gathers no _____.

5. A stitch in time saves _____.

6. A leopard cannot change its _____.

7. An apple a day keeps the doctor _____.

8. Absence makes the heart grow _____.

9. Actions speak louder than _____.

10. All good things must come to an _____.

11. All is fair in love and _____.

12. All that glitters is not _____.

13. All's well that ends _____.

14. Bad news travels _____.

15. Beauty is only skin _____.

16. Better late than _____.

17. Birds of a feather flock _____.

18. Blood is thicker than _____.

19. Beauty is in the eye of the _____.

20. Charity begins at _____.

21. Crime does not _____.

22. Curiosity killed the _____.

23. Don't count your chickens before they _____.

24. Don't cut off your nose to spite your _____.

25. Don't put all your eggs in one _____.

26. Don't wash your dirty linen in _____.

27. Easier said than _____.

28. Experience is the best _____.

29. Give the devil his _____.

30. God helps those who help _____.

31. Good fences make good _____.

32. Familiarity breeds _____.

33. Finders keepers, losers _____.

34. Great minds think _____.

35. Honesty is the best _____.

36. Ignorance is _____.

37. It's no use crying over spilt _____.

38. It takes two to _____.

39. Live and let _____.

40. Laughter is the best _____.

Memory Booster

Do not deliberate your responses. Go with your gut instinct and move through the list at a brisk pace. If you get stuck, skip the item and keep going. Quickly go through the list a second time to try to complete any items you missed.

41. Let sleeping dogs _____.

42. Let the buyer _____.

43. Life is just a bowl of _____.

44. Like father, like _____.

45. Look before you _____.

46. Love conquers _____.

47. Money is the root of all _____.

48. Nothing is certain except death and _____.

49. Nothing succeeds like _____.

50. Nothing ventured, nothing _____.

51. Necessity is the mother of _____.

52. No news is good _____.

53. No pain, no _____.

54. Old habits die _____.

55. Opportunity seldom knocks _____.

56. Practice makes _____.

57. Seeing is _____.

58. Silence is _____.

59. Still waters run _____.

60. Strike while the iron is _____.

61. The early bird catches the _____.

62. The best things in life are _____.

63. There is no honor among _____.

64. There is safety in _____.

65. The end justifies the _____.

66. The first step is the _____.

67. The grass is always greener on the other side of the _____.

68. The more you get the more you _____.

69. The proof of the pudding is in the _____.

70. There are always two sides of a _____.

71. There's no smoke without _____.

72. To err is human; to forgive is _____.

73. Tomorrow is another _____.

74. Too many cooks spoil the _____.

75. There's no fool like an old _____.

76. Time and tide wait for _____.

77. Those who live in glass houses should not throw _____.

78. Time heals all _____.

79. Two heads are better than _____.

80. Two is company and three is a _____.

81. Variety is the spice of _____.

82. Virtue is its own _____.

83. When in doubt do _____.

84. Where there's a will there's a _____.

85. You can't judge a book by its _____.

Memory Assessment

Needs improvement: Gave fewer than 30 correct responses

Average: Gave 30-39 correct responses

Good: Gave 40-59 correct responses

Very good: Gave 60-70 correct responses

Excellent: Gave more than 70 correct responses

Who Am I?

How to Play

Below are a series of clues that will lead you to recall the name of a famous historical person or celebrity. Once you've put the together the clues, your challenge will be to call up the name. (Answers are on page 144.)

1. I was a female American aviator who mysteriously disappeared over the Pacific Ocean during a navigational flight in 1937: _____

2. I was a famous American gangster in 1920s and 1930s. Some people called me "Scarface": _____

3. I am an American female singer of gospel, soul, and R&B born in Memphis in 1942. Some people call me the "Queen of Soul." "Respect" is one of my signature songs: _____

4. My career in nursing began in 1851 and I considered it a divine calling. I am remembered today as a pioneer of modern nursing because of the compassionate care, administrative skills, and medical record-keeping I introduced into the profession of nursing: _____

5. I am an African-American religious leader, political activist, and active in the civil rights movement. I was a candidate for the democratic nomination in the 1984 presidential election: _____

6. When I was 19 months old, I was left with severe disabilities as a result of fever. I lost my ability to communicate at an early developmental age and became quite unmanageable. My teacher's first task was to instill discipline: _____

7. I am a female country singer who became famous at the age of 13 with the hit song "Blue." My most recognized crossover hit is "How Do I Live," which according to the Billboard charts is one of the most successful songs in music history: _____

8. I was a national icon who led the struggle for India's independence from British colonial rule, empowered by tens of millions of common Indians. I abhorred any form of terrorism or violence: _____

9. I was a retired African-American seamstress and figure in the American Civil Rights movement, most famous for my refusal in 1955 to give up my bus seat to a white man: _____

Memory Booster

If the name is on the tip of your tongue, but you can't pull it up, try one of the memory-boosting techniques below:

- If a letter from the alphabet floats into your mind, trust this brain clue. Your brain files names through first-letter association, so there's a good chance the name is associated with this letter or a similar sound. Close your eyes, relax your mind, and go with the clue.

- If you feel certain you know who the person is, but can't quite grasp the name, here are two more strategies:
- Close your eyes and visualize the person in as much detail as possible.
- State out loud any and all facts you can recall related to the person.

10. I am one of the most popular and controversial white, male rap singers. My LP *The Slim Shady*, released in 1999, went triple platinum by the end of the year. I was brought to fame by rapper/producer Dr. Dre: _____

11. I attended classes at Le Cordon Bleu in Paris. I am a famous American cook, author, and television personality who introduced French cuisine and cooking techniques to America: _____

12. I became a migrant farm worker at the age of 10, with the rest of my family, when we lost our farm during the Great Depression. In 1965, I led a strike of California grape pickers in demand of higher wages along with a national boycott of California table grapes. I became an American labor rights hero for supporting the rights of Mexican migrant farm workers: _____

13. I was a United States astronaut in the early days of the space program. On July 20, 1969, along with fellow astronaut Buzz Aldrin, I landed the *Apollo 11* lunar module *Eagle* on the Moon. Upon taking my first step onto the moon, I said, "That's one small step for a man, one giant leap for mankind": _____

14. I was an Irish American actress who won an Academy Award as best actress in the film *The Country Girl*. In 1956, I married Prince Rainier Grimaldi III. I died when my car went off the road on the cliffs of Monaco: _____

15. I was a French aristocrat and writer of philosophy in the 1800s. I was a philosopher of extreme freedom, unrestrained by morality, religion, or law, with the pursuit of personal pleasure being the highest principle. I was incarcerated in various prisons and in an insane asylum for about 32 years of my life. The term "sadism" is derived from my name: _____

16. I was a famous American baseball player and national icon inducted into the Baseball Hall of Fame. My record number of home runs was 60 in the 1927 season. My nicknames were "The Bambino" and "The Sultan of Swat": _____

17. I am an Academy Award-winning English actor, singer and author, best known for my starring roles in the films *Mary Poppins* and *The Sound of Music*: _____

18. I am the final prophet of Islam. Islam is considered by Muslims to be the final step in the revelation of a monotheist religion of which earlier versions were the teachings of Moses, Jesus, and other prophets: _____

19. I was an American jurist and first African-American to serve on the United States Supreme Court: _____

20. I am a Russian-born professional tennis player. In 2004 I became the second youngest Wimbleton women's champion by defeating two-time defending champion Serena Williams in straight sets. I continue to play professional tennis and, in 2003, I signed a modeling contract with IMJ models: _____

Memory Assessment

Needs improvement: Gave 1–4 correct responses

Average: Gave 5–7 correct responses

Good: Gave 8–10 correct responses

Very good: Gave 11–15 correct responses

Excellent: Gave more than 15 correct responses

What Am I?

How to Play

In this game, you will be presented with a series of definitions of common terms. Your memory challenge is to use the definition to recall the correct term. (Answers are on page 144.)

1. A form of football in which the ball may be kicked or bounced off any part of the body except for the arms and hands: _____
2. A tube through which a swimmer can breathe while moving facedown at or just below the surface of the water: _____
3. Subnormal body temperature that can result from prolonged exposure to freezing weather conditions: _____
4. A division of a poem consisting of a series of lines arranged in a recurring pattern of meter and rhyme: _____
5. A governmental document issued to a citizen, authenticating the bearer's identity and right to travel to other countries: _____
6. A contract renting property to another for a specified time period in consideration for rent: _____

7. The exclusive right guaranteed to an inventor to manufacture or sell an invention for a specified number of years: _____
8. A canvas sheet attached by springs to a frame used for tumbling and jumping: _____
9. The poisonous fluid secreted by some snakes and introduced into the victim by biting: _____
10. An overreaction of the immune system to ordinarily harmless substances resulting in symptoms such as a skin rash or sneezing: _____
11. A corpse used by medical students for dissection: _____
12. The art of ornamental needlework: _____
13. A frozen dessert made from iced fruit puree, often used to cleanse one's palate between courses in a meal: _____

Memory Assessment

Needs improvement: Gave 1-4 correct responses

Average: Gave 5-7 correct responses

Good: Gave 8-10 correct responses

Excellent: Gave 11-13 correct responses

Memory Booster

If you experience the "tip of the tongue" phenomenon, here are some helpful memory tips:

- Because anxiety interferes with memory, close your eyes and relax your mind. Many times the word will "float" to the surface.
- Try an alphabetic search. Try out each letter of the alphabet as the beginning of the word you are seeking.
- State out loud any facts or personal associations that come to mind. Often these will trigger your memory of the word.
- If your mind keeps presenting words beginning with a specific letter, there is a good reason. Go with the clue your memory is surfacing.

Famous Quotations

How to Play

You will be presented with a series of quotes from famous people. Your challenge is to match each quote with its original speaker. When you are finished, check your responses against the answer key on page 144.

Quotations

1. "The game isn't over until it's over."
2. "All the world's a stage, and all the men and women merely players."
3. "Anyone who has never made a mistake has never tried anything new."
4. "Glory is fleeting, but obscurity is forever."
5. "Give me a museum and I'll fill it."
6. "God is a comedian playing to an audience too afraid to laugh."
7. "If you can count your money, you don't have a billion dollars."
8. "Once you eliminate the impossible, whatever remains, no matter how improbable, must be true."
9. "We didn't lose the game; we just ran out of time."
10. "A friendship founded on business is better than a business founded on friendship."
11. "I love Mickey Mouse more than any woman I have ever known."
12. "There are people in the world so hungry, that God cannot appear to them except in the form of bread."
13. "Ask not what your country can do for you, but what you can do for your country."
14. "Not only is there no God, but try finding a plumber on Sunday."
15. "I have never let my schooling interfere with my education."

Speakers

A. Mark Twain
B. Walt Disney
C. John F. Kennedy
D. Mahatma Gandhi
E. Vince Lombardi
F. Yogi Berra
G. John D. Rockefeller
H. Woody Allen
I. Voltaire
J. J. Paul Getty
K. Pablo Picasso
L. Napoleon Bonaparte
M. Sherlock Holmes (Sir Arthur Conan Doyle)
N. Albert Einstein
O. William Shakespeare

Memory Booster

If you don't recognize a quote or its speaker, try applying some deductive reasoning. For example, if you see a quote about the stars and universe, you might deduce that the speaker is Carl Sagan, the famous astronomer.

Memory Assessment

Needs improvement: Made 1-7 correct matches

Average: Made 8-10 correct matches

Good: Made 11-12 correct matches

Very good: Made 13-14 correct matches

Excellent: Made 15 correct matches

Around the World

How to Play

You will be presented with a list of world capitals and a list of the countries in which they are found. Your long-term memory challenge is to match each capital with its correct country. When you are finished, check your responses against the answer key on pages 144–145.

Capitals

1. Kabul
2. Phnom Penh
3. Bogotá
4. Beijing
5. Havana
6. Cairo
7. New Delhi
8. Tehran
9. Baghdad
10. Tokyo
11. Hanoi
12. Oslo
13. Stockholm
14. Moscow
15. Pretoria
16. Jerusalem
17. Beirut
18. Berlin
19. Dublin
20. Copenhagen

Countries

A. Vietnam
B. Japan
C. Russia
D. Israel
E. Egypt
F. Lebanon
G. Germany
H. Iraq
I. Norway
J. Afghanistan
K. Cambodia
L. Colombia
M. Sweden
N. China
O. Cuba
P. India
Q. Iran
R. Ireland
S. Denmark
T. South Africa

Famous Places

How to Play

You will be presented with famous places and the countries where they are found. Your long-term memory challenge is to match each famous place with its correct country. When you have finished, check your responses against the answer key on page 145.

Famous Places

1. Mayan ruins
2. Great Wall
3. Red Square
4. Stonehenge
5. Taj Mahal
6. Sphinx and the pyramids
7. Cliffs of Moher
8. Matterhorn
9. Fjords
10. Grand Canyon
11. Parthenon
12. Mount Everest
13. Coliseum
14. Wailing Wall
15. Eiffel Tower
16. Rock of Gibraltar
17. Sahara
18. Statue of Trojan horse

Location

A. Turkey
B. India
C. Italy
D. England
E. China
F. Israel
G. France
H. Nepal and Tibet
I. United States
J. Norway
K. Greece
L. Ireland
M. Switzerland and Italy
N. Yucatán Peninsula
O. Russia
P. Northern Africa
Q. Iberian Peninsula
R. Egypt

Memory Assessment

Needs improvement: Made 1-7 correct matches

Average: Made 8-10 correct matches

Good: Made 11-13 correct matches

Very good: Made 14-16 correct matches

Excellent: Made 17-18 correct matches

What Do You Know?

The following multiple-choice quiz will draw on information you've learned about memory over time. It will also increase your knowledge about how memory works and important lifestyle factors that affect memory. Select the correct responses. When you've completed the quiz, go to page 145.

1. Your memory is practically guaranteed to slip a little as you get older.
   A. True   B. False

2. As you age, there's not much you can do to improve your memory.
   A. True   B. False

3. Which of these is a clear sign of a serious memory problem?
   A. Forgetting where you parked your car
   B. Losing your car keys
   C. Temporarily forgetting a common word
   D. None of the above

4. Which of these is a sign of normal age-related memory loss?
   A. Finding yourself unable to do a routine task, like setting the table
   B. Forgetting how to balance your checkbook
   C. Having trouble finding familiar places when driving
   D. Needing extra time to do calculations in your head

5. When a person develops Alzheimer's disease, short-term memory is the first to go.
   A. True   B. False

6. Which of these conditions can cause reversible memory loss?
   A. Thyroid hormone deficiency
   B. Depression
   C. Vitamin B12 deficiency
   D. All of the above

7. Heavy alcohol use can lead to Korsakoff's syndrome, a condition that destroys a person's ability to store new information.
   A. True   B. False

8. Which of the following beverages has been shown in clinical studies to boost memory after consumption?
   A. Red wine
   B. Sports drinks
   C. Coffee
   D. Lemonade

9. Which of these activities has been shown in clinical studies to interfere with memory?
   A. Talking on a cell phone
   B. Multitasking
   C. Power napping
   D. Eating chocolate

10. Most people over age sixty-five have some form of Alzheimer's disease.
    A. True   B. False

11. Which of the following has been clinically shown to reduce memory capacity?
    A. Not getting a good night's sleep
    B. Pigging out on sweets
    C. Pets in the home
    D. Using scented laundry detergents

12. Which of the following activities boosts memory?
    A. Aerobic exercise
    B. Eating foods high in antioxidants such as dark-colored fruits and vegetables
    C. Mental exercises
    D. All of the above

Memory Chargers

Here are some fun follow-up actions you can take to practice retrieving information through the processes of recall and recognition.

1. Play games and watch television game shows such as *Jeopardy* that stimulate retrieval of information through recall.

2. Play games and watch television shows such as *Who Wants to Be a Millionaire* that stimulate retrieval of information through recognition.

3. Do crossword puzzles. If you're not a pro, get the easy editions with the answers in the back. If you get stuck, look up the answer and then continue to play.

4. Ask your librarian or retail bookseller for books that ask you to find antonyms and synonyms of common words. This is a great activity for word recall. Alternatively, have a friend make up lists of verbs, adjectives, adverbs, and nouns. Then challenge yourself to come up with an antonym and synonym for each word on the list. Antonyms are words that have opposite meanings. For example, an antonym for the word "elated" is "dejected." Synonyms are words that have the same or a similar meaning. For example, a word that is the same as or similar to "brave" is "courageous."

5. Get math flash cards and see how fast you can come up with the correct answers. Time yourself. Each time you play, try to beat your last time.

6. Make up your own recall flash cards. Using index cards, write a different theme on each card. Examples of themes include dance styles, recent movies, best-selling books, presidents, famous scientists, mountain ranges, and the like. Get a timer that can be set for seconds, a piece of scrap paper, and a pencil. Set the timer for 30 seconds and select your first theme flash card. Write down all the items you can think of that fit the theme. When the timer goes off, put your pencil down. The goal is to come up with as many items as possible in the allotted time frame. This is a fun, competitive game to play with friends and family. You can play one person against another or as teams. The individual or team that comes up with the greatest number of items in 30 seconds wins the round. If you are playing with partners or in teams, you might want to increase the time limit.

Attention, Please!

I have a photographic memory, but once in a while I forget to take off the lens cap.

—*Milton Berle*

Acquiring an A+ Memory

In Lessons Three and Four, you used the mental activities of recall and recognition to retrieve information from your working memory and your long-term memory. Your ability to retrieve a memory depends on how well the memory is laid down in the first place. The laying down of memories is called *encoding*. Encoding a memory works a little like a computer that uses RAM (random-access memory) for the temporary storage of information before it is placed in the hard drive for long-term storage. Now, in the final lessons of *Supercharge Your Memory!* you'll focus on the memory process of encoding. You'll see how proven memory techniques that complement the three learning styles can help boost your brain's ability to store and retrieve memories.

Shallow Encoding

Laying down a short-term, working memory involves *shallow encoding*. The most common type of shallow encoding involves repeating information to ourselves using our inner voice. A good example of this is remembering a phone number the operator gives us. A higher order of shallow encoding involves using an inner *visuospatial* sketch pad. Notice how each of these memory processes correlates with the auditory (hearing) and visual (seeing) learning styles discussed in Lesson Two.

Elaborative Encoding

Laying down a memory through *elaborative encoding* helps transfer the memory from working memory to the more secure and lasting storage bins of long-term memory.

Elaborative encoding is the mental glue that makes memories stick. The best approach to elaborative encoding is to *associate* the information to be remembered with something already in your memory, thereby making the information more meaningful and memorable. So how does this connective glue work? The glue consists of one part *attention* and one part *association* . . . and it is the foundation of an A+ memory.

In Lessons Five and Six, you'll learn how to make your own memory glue by drawing on a combination of learning styles as you engage in a series of attention- and association-boosting games.

A Is for "Attention"

You learn something every day if you pay attention.

—Ray LeBlond

A is for "attention." The first step in creating an A+ memory is learning how to focus in the moment. Paying attention requires being present. Unfortunately, most of us are rarely ever present. We are rushing about and our minds are cluttered with worries about what we didn't do in the past and what we must do in the future. Is it any wonder that we can't remember what is happening in the moment? Common memory complaints ("Where did I park my car?" or "Where did I put my wallet?") are directly attributable to a lack of in-the-moment attentiveness.

Being present is a conscious choice, and active observation is the art of paying attention. Active observation involves using our five senses (taste, touch, smell, hearing, and sight) to experience a present moment. Activating our five senses not only improves our attention but also enriches our lives, allowing us to experience each moment to the fullest.

The biggest challenge to paying attention in the twenty-first century is multitasking. The brain, unlike a computer, is not designed to multitask. To switch gears, the brain must literally stop, start, and retrigger each time there is an interruption. This causes fragmented concentration, resulting in memory inefficiencies as well as increased stress and poor-quality work. Multitasking at home and at work has been linked, in recent scientific studies, to a bad night's sleep as the brain tries to recapture the many memory fragments from a day filled with mental starts and stops. Sleep deprivation is a known contributor to memory inefficiencies.

So how well do you pay attention when it comes to making memories? You'll find out in the next series of fun and challenging games as you learn how to make memories stick by applying attention-boosting memory techniques.

Autopilot

How to Play

How well do you focus on the things you see every day? Find out by answering the questions below. (Answers are on page 146.)

1. What president's face is on a five-dollar bill?

2. What is the shape of a stop sign (how many sides)?

3. What color is Ronald McDonald's hair?

4. Where is your cell phone right now?

5. What is the order of the colors on a traffic light from bottom to top?

6. What are the traditional colors on a Dunkin' Donuts sign?

7. How many light switches are in your home or apartment?

8. In a fine restaurant, is the bread plate to the left or right of the dinner plate?

9. What two warning signs tell you to stop your vehicle when a school bus is picking up or letting off children?

10. What is the number of cards in a standard deck of playing cards (minus the jokers)?

11. How many white stripes are on an American flag?

12. How many *R*s are on a railroad-crossing sign?

13. What is the color of your boss's eyes?

14. On a U.S. license plate, is the state name above or below the license plate number?

15. On either side of a handicapped parking space, are the lines restricting parking horizontal, vertical, or diagonal?

Memory Booster

For questions involving visually stored memories, close your eyes and try to reproduce the image in your mind's eye. For questions that have an experiential learning component, feel yourself engaged in the action. For question seven, you might feel yourself walking through the rooms in your apartment flicking on each light switch.

Memory Assessment

Needs improvement: Gave 1-4 correct responses

Average: Gave 5-7 correct responses

Good: Gave 8-10 correct responses

Very good: Gave 11-13 correct responses

Excellent: Gave 14-15 correct responses

Unfocused Reader

How to Play

Read each of the phrases below one at a time. After you have read each phrase, cover it with a piece of paper or your hand and write down the phrase as you remember it. Upon completion, wait 15 seconds. Then go back and read each phrase again out loud, concentrating on each word in the phrase. What did you discover? (Answer on page 146.)

THE GRASS
IS ALWAYS GREENER ON
ON THE OTHER SIDE

A BIRD
IN THE HAND IS
IS WORTH TWO IN
THE BUSH

ALL IS FAIR
IN LOVE AND
AND WAR

STRIKE
WHILE THE
THE IRON IS HOT

Memory Assessment

Needs improvement: Got it by the fourth phrase

Average: Got it by the third phrase

Good: Got it by the second phrase

Excellent: Got it by the first phrase

Focused Reader

How to Play

Read each excerpt. Allow 3 minutes to complete the reading, then answer the questions. (Answers are on page 146.)

Excerpt One: *The Adventures of Huckleberry Finn,* by Mark Twain

Now the way that the book winds up is this: Tom and me found the money that the robbers hid in the cave, and it made us rich. We got six thousand dollars apiece—all gold. It was an awful sight of money when it was piled up. Well, Judge Thatcher he took it and put it out at interest, and it fetched us a dollar a day apiece all the year round—more than a body could tell what to do with. The Widow Douglas she took me for her son, and allowed she would sivilize me; but it was rough living in the house all the time, considering how dismal regular and decent the widow was in all her ways; and so when I couldn't stand it no longer I lit out. I got into my old rags and my sugar-hogshead again, and was free and satisfied. But Tom Sawyer he hunted me up and said he was going to start a band of robbers, and I might join if I would go back to the widow and be respectable. So I went back.

Answer the following questions about the excerpt from memory:

1. Where did Huck and Tom find the stolen money?
2. What currency was the money in?
3. How much interest did the money earn a day?
4. What is the name of the person who wants to adopt Huck as her son?
5. What two types of clothing did Huck wear when he ran away?
6. Why did Huck return to the widow after running away?

Memory Assessment

Needs improvement: Answered 1-2 questions correctly

Average: Answered 3-4 questions correctly

Good: Answered 5 questions correctly

Excellent: Answered 6 questions correctly

Memory Booster

As you read each excerpt, imagine that you are a reporter who will be called upon to recall the important facts related in the text. Be prepared to answer questions about *who, what, where, when, why,* and *how many.* Actively engaging in what you read by asking yourself questions boosts memory. Physically underlining key words and phrases helps visual and experiential learners retain information.

Excerpt Two: *The Life and Adventures of Robinson Crusoe,* by Daniel Defoe

I was born in the year 1632, in the city of York, of a good family. . . . Being the third son of the family and not bred to any trade, my head began to be filled very early with rambling thoughts: my father, who was very ancient, had given me a competent share of learning, as far as house-education and a country free-school generally go, and designed me for the law; but I would be satisfied with nothing but going to sea; and my inclination to this led me so strongly, against the will, nay, the commands of my father, and against all the entreaties and persuasions of my mother and other friends, that there seemed to be something fatal in the propensity of nature tending directly to the life of misery which was to befall me. . . .
It was not till almost a year after this that I broke loose, though, in the meantime, I continued obstinately deaf to all proposals of settling to business, and frequently expostulated with my father and mother about their being so positively determined against what they knew my inclinations prompted me to. But being one day at Hull, where I went casually, and without any purpose of making an elopement at that time; but, I say, being there, and one of my companions being about to sail to London, in his father's ship, and prompting me to go with them with the common allurement of seafaring men, that it should cost me nothing for my passage, I consulted neither father nor mother anymore, nor so much as sent them word of it; but leaving them to hear of it as they might . . . I went on board a ship bound for London.

Answer the following questions about the excerpt from memory.

1. In what year was Robinson Crusoe born?
2. What word describes the age of his father?
3. What was the extent of Robinson Crusoe's education?
4. What profession did Robinson Crusoe's father wish him to pursue?
5. What type of life was to befall him?
6. How much time passed before Robinson Crusoe made his elopement?
7. Where did Robinson Crusoe set sail for on his first voyage?
8. What was the cost of the passage?
9. On whose boat did he sail?
10. What word did he leave his parents regarding his departure?

Memory Assessment

Needs improvement: Answered 1-2 questions correctly

Average: Answered 3-4 questions correctly

Good: Answered 5-6 questions correctly

Very good: Answered 7-8 questions correctly

Excellent: Answered 9-10 questions correctly

Compare and Contrast

How to Play

Jungle Mania

You will be presented with three sets of "twin" pictures. The twin pictures will appear identical on the surface; however, when you focus your attention on the details, you will notice that the twin pictures contain slight variations. Your challenge is to spot the ten details in the picture on the right that make it different from the picture on the left in less than 3 minutes. (Answers are on page 146.)

Memory Booster

First scan the drawings as a whole to see if any differences jump out at you. Then hunt for differences in the details. You can do this by segmenting the drawings into quarters or segmenting the pictures by specific types of details (e.g., leaves, vase, petals, etc.). Each time you look at the drawings from a different perspective, you are using a new visual lens through which to capture new and unseen details.

Memory Assessment

Needs improvement: Identified 1-2 differences

Average: Identified 3-4 differences

Good: Identified 5-6 differences

Very good: Identified 7-8 differences

Excellent: Identified 9-10 differences

Abstract Artist

Memory Skills:
Attention

Memory Process:
Recall

Challenge Level:

How to Play

You will be presented with three different abstract designs. Study each design for 3 minutes. Then cover the design and try to reproduce it from memory. Before reproducing the design from memory, you may find it helpful to actually practice drawing the design on scrap paper while looking at the design. The challenge is to reproduce the main structure and as many details as you can. Artistic skill is not important.

Design One

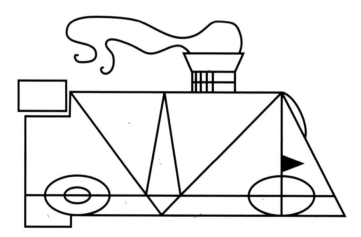

Memory Assessment

Needs improvement: Re-created less than 25 percent of details and main structure

Average: Re-created 25 percent of details and main structure

Good: Re-created 50 percent of details and main structure

Very good: Re-created 75 percent of details and main structure

Excellent: Re-created more than 75 percent of details and main structure

Design Two

Study the abstract design for 3 minutes. Then cover the design and reproduce it on a piece of scrap paper. When you are finished, compare your design with the original.

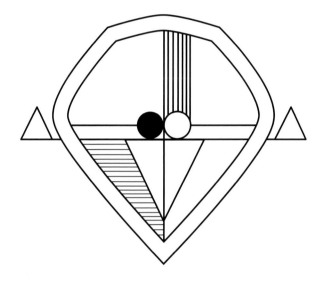

Memory Booster

Look for repeatable patterns and familiar shapes. Try to associate elements of each design with things your memory already knows and recognizes. For instance, a squiggly line might look like the tail of a mouse. The overall shape of the design might remind you of an umbrella. The more meaning you can give to the design through familiar associations, the more memory glue you create.

Memory Assessment

Needs improvement: Re-created less than 25 percent of details and main structure

Average: Re-created 25 percent of details and main structure

Good: Re-created 50 percent of details and main structure

Very good: Re-created 75 percent of details and main structure

Excellent: Re-created more than 75 percent of details and main structure

Design Three

Study the abstract design for 3 minutes. Then cover the design and reproduce it on a piece of scrap paper. When you are finished, compare your design with the original.

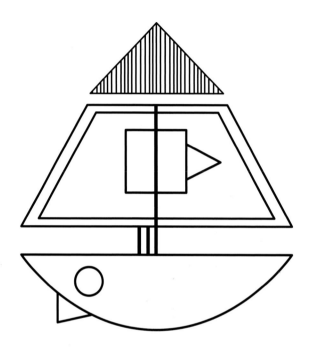

Spatial Patterns

How to Play

You will be presented with four spatial patterns. Your challenge is to study each pattern and then identify the original pattern among a group of imposters. See how quickly you can spot the original.

Pattern One

Study the pattern for 10 seconds. Then look at the next page.

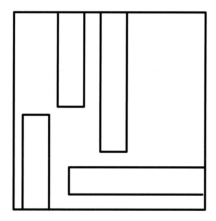

Memory Booster

Look for unique characteristics associated with the pattern. Notice the physical orientation among the shapes. Use spatial references. Are angles or shapes pointing up, down, or diagonally? Can you detect any north, south, east, or west clues that will help you lay down a memory of the pattern? Are the shapes themselves fat, skinny, pointy, or rounded?

Which one of the following patterns did you see on the previous page? Put an X to the left of the original pattern.

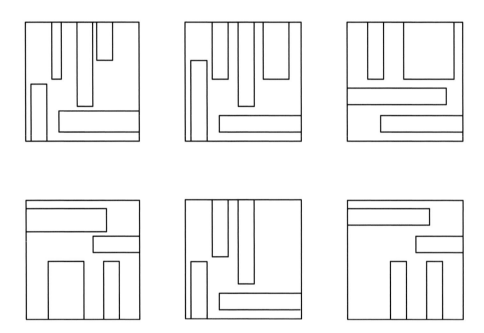

Pattern Two
Study the pattern for 10 seconds. Then look at the next page.

Which one of the following have you just looked at? Put an X to the left of the original pattern.

Pattern Three

Study the pattern for 10 seconds. Then look at the next page.

Which one of the following patterns did you see on the previous page? Put an X above the original pattern.

Pattern Four

Study the pattern for 10 seconds. Then look at the next page.

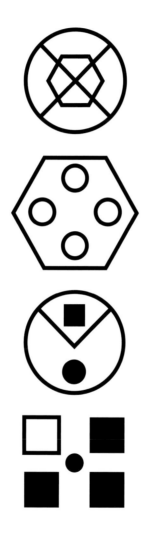

Which one of the following patterns did you see on the previous page? Put an X to the left of the original pattern.

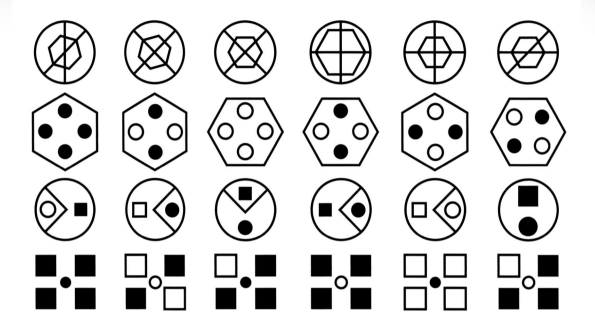

Mixed-Bag Patterns

How to Play

You will be presented with two sets of graphics consisting of a mixed bag of familiar numbers, letters, and shapes arranged in a particular spatial orientation. Study each set of mixed-bag graphics; then go to the next page and answer the questions. (Answers are on page 147.)

Set One

Study the details for 3 minutes; then look at the next page.

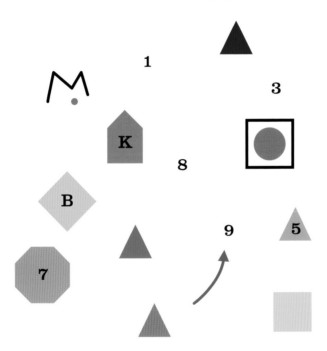

Memory Booster

The more actively we engage with the information to be remembered, the more vivid the memories will be. Using your finger, trace the path from one object to the next. Touch each shape and say its name out loud. Touch each number and letter as you say its name out loud. Notice the physical orientation of the shapes, numbers, and letters on the page. Ask yourself questions about the objects in the pattern. How many numbers, letters, and shapes are there individually and in total? Are the numbers odd or even? Are the letters uppercase or lowercase? Are the letters vowels or consonants?

Answer the questions about the details on the preceding page.

1. What is the only even number?

2. What letter is inside the pentagon?

3. The circle is inside what other shape?

4. How many triangles are there?

5. The arrow is pointing to which number?

6. What number is inside one of the triangles?

7. What letter is inside the diamond?

8. Inside which shape is the number 7?

9. How many circles appear?

10. What letter has a colored dot immediately below it?

11. What color is the circle?

12. What color is the arrow?

Memory Assessment

Needs improvement: Answered 1-2 questions correctly

Average: Answered 3-4 questions correctly

Good: Answered 5-7 questions correctly

Very good: Answered 8-10 questions correctly

Excellent: Answered 11-12 questions correctly

Set Two

Study the details for 3 minutes; then answer the questions on the next page.

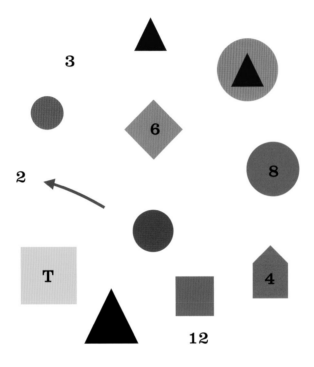

Answer the questions about the details on the preceding page.

1. Which is the only odd number?

2. What number is inside the diamond?

3. The triangle is inside what other shape?

4. The arrow is pointing to which number?

5. How many circles are there?

6. What number is inside the red circle?

7. What letter is inside the square?

8. Inside which shape is the number 4?

9. How many triangles are there?

10. What number has a colored green square above it?

11. Name the color of one of the triangles.

12. Name the color of one of the circles.

Memory Assessment

Needs improvement: Answered 1-2 questions correctly

Average: Answered 3-4 questions correctly

Good: Answered 5-7 questions correctly

Very good: Answered 8-10 questions correctly

Excellent: Answered 11-12 questions correctly

Out and About

How to Play

You will be presented with four dynamic outdoor scenes you might encounter when you are out and about. Study each scene for 3 minutes. Then go to the next page and answer the questions that follow.

Memory Booster

Memory attention increases when you get actively involved in what you want to remember. Ask yourself questions about the actions in each scene. Who is in the scene, what are they doing, and where are they? To prompt your thinking and recall, ask yourself questions related to the five Ws: who, what, where, when, and why. Imagine that you are actually in the scene, involved in the action. Choose a character in the scene and be that person. To heighten your focus, add an emotional element. Imagine that a crime is about to take place and that you will be asked to give an accounting to the police.

Scene One: On the Farm

Answer the following questions about the farm scene. (See page 147 for answers.)

1. What two animals in the scene are not domestic farm animals?

2. Is the farmer wearing a hat?

3. What is on top of the barn?

4. What two clues tell you the time of day?

5. What direction are the sheep on the hill facing?

6. What structure is in the foreground of the scene?

7. What tool is leaning against the barn?

8. What is the farmer doing?

9. What is growing in the field?

10. What is swimming in the pond?

Scene Two: At the Beach

Study the scene below for 3 minutes. Then go to the next page and answer the questions.

Answer the following questions about the beach scene. (See page 147 for answers.)

1. Who is not barefoot?

2. What are the clues that tell you it is a windy day?

3. Is the child buried in the sand a boy or a girl?

4. Are the birds all flying in the same direction?

5. How many coconuts are on the palm tree?

6. Name three objects from the sea that are lying on the sand.

7. How many people are building a sand castle?

8. What are the people in the water doing?

9. What is the man reading?

10. What is the child eating?

(See page 147 for answers.)

Memory Assessment

Needs improvement: Answered 1-2 questions correctly

Average: Answered 3-4 questions correctly

Good: Answered 5-6 questions correctly

Very good: Answered 7-8 questions correctly

Excellent: Answered 9-10 questions correctly

Scene Three: City Slicker

Study the scene below for 2 minutes. Then go to the next page and answer the questions.

Answer the following questions about the city scene. (See page 147 for answers.)

1. What is the number on the bus?

2. What store has a sale sign in the window?

3. What modes of transportation are not motorized?

4. What outerwear is the woman walking the dog wearing?

5. What is the dog doing?

6. Which way is the jogger running?

7. How many people are in the taxi?

8. What is the man throwing away in the garbage can?

9. What is the policeman signaling?

10. What appears on the horizon?

(See page 147 for answers.)

Memory Assessment

Needs improvement: Answered 1–2 questions correctly

Average: Answered 3–4 questions correctly

Good: Answered 5–6 questions correctly

Very good: Answered 7–8 questions correctly

Excellent: Answered 9–10 questions correctly

Scene Four: Central Park

Study the scene below for 3 minutes. Then go to the next page and answer the questions.

Answer the following questions about the park scene. (See page 147 for answers.)

1. Where does the path lead?

2. How many dogs is the dog walker walking?

3. What does the sign by the pond say?

4. Who is wearing glasses?

5. What is the hairstyle of the girls on the swing?

6. What is the policeman's mode of transportation?

7. Where is the water fountain in relation to the sandbox?

8. What is the man on the park bench doing?

9. What board game is being played?

10. How many swans are in the pond?

Memory Assessment

Needs improvement: Answered 1–2 questions correctly

Average: Answered 3–4 questions correctly

Good: Answered 5–6 questions correctly

Very good: Answered 7–8 questions correctly

Excellent: Answered 9–10 questions correctly

Make It; Grow It

How to Play

Below are three sets of written instructions. Read the instructions carefully; then answer the questions that follow.

Set One: How to Make Sweet Potato Casserole

Study the recipe ingredients. Then go to the next page and answer the questions.

Sweet Potato Casserole

2 packages dried apricots
3 cups hot water
2 cans sweet potatoes
¾ cup brown sugar

3 tablespoons butter, melted
3 teaspoons orange juice
Marshmallows

Soak apricots in hot water for 1 hour. Simmer apricot-water mixture for 40 minutes; then drain, saving liquid. Mix apricots until mushy. Cut sweet potatoes into ½-inch strips. Put a layer of sweet potatoes in the bottom of a greased casserole; cover with apricots; then sprinkle with some of the brown sugar. Repeat these layers. Mix butter with orange juice and apricot liquid and pour over all. Bake at 375 degrees for 35 minutes. Dot with marshmallows and return to oven for 5 more minutes.

Memory Booster

Read the instructions out loud, visualizing yourself actively engaged in each activity. The first and third sets of instructions are recipes. See yourself laying out the ingredients on the counter. Activate your senses. Hear the eggs cracking open; see the yolk spilling out; feel the grittiness of the salt between your fingers; smell the scent of vanilla. The second set of instructions involves growing something in your garden. Use your imagination to make each step come alive in your mind.

Answer the following questions. (Answers are on page 147.)

1. What are the three liquids you will use in the recipe?

2. What is the consistency of the apricots required for the recipe?

3. What is the size of the sweet potato strips?

4. What is the sequence of the three layers in the casserole dish from bottom to top?

5. What oven temperature is required for cooking?

6. What is the total length of the cooking time?

7. What is the final ingredient added before serving?

Memory Assessment

Needs improvement: Answered 1-2 questions correctly

Average: Answered 3-4 questions correctly

Good: Answered 5 questions correctly

Very good: Answered 6 questions correctly

Excellent: Answered 7 questions correctly

Set Two: How to Grow Pumpkins

Carefully read the instructions out loud. Then go to the next page and answer the questions.

1. Buy pumpkin plants at the nursery. Otherwise, start seeds indoors about three weeks before the last expected frost.

2. Choose a site that gets full sun and has soil with a pH of 6.0 to 6.8. Pumpkins need light and very rich soil that drains well.

3. Cultivate your pumpkin patch by plowing each row deep and wide: Both roots and vines can spread as far as 15 feet in all directions.

4. Harden off the seedlings, whether store-bought or homegrown, and transfer them to the garden when all danger of frost has passed.

5. Plant them in hills, setting them at least as deep as they were in the pots.

6. Allow at least 5 feet between plants in each direction.

7. Mulch with organic matter once plants are established to conserve moisture and deter weeds.

8. Use cloches or floating covers to protect young plants from chilly winds.

9. Make sure the plants get 1 to 2 inches of water per week, especially when they're blooming and setting fruit.

10. Feed plants with compost tea or seaweed extract every two or three weeks.

11. Pinch vines back to limit their growth once fruits appear.

12. Rotate pumpkins once in a while to keep them symmetrical.

13. Place boards under large pumpkins to keep them from rotting.

14. Harvest orange pumpkins after the vines have shriveled and died, but before the first hard freeze.

Answer the following questions. (Answers are on page 147.)

1. Why do you rotate pumpkins while they are growing?
2. What do you feed growing pumpkins?
3. How do you keep large pumpkins from rotting?
4. What type of weather is harmful to growing pumpkins?
5. How much space should you allow between pumpkin plants?
6. How far can pumpkin roots and vines potentially spread?
7. How much water should pumpkin plants get weekly when blooming and setting fruit?
8. What is the ideal soil pH for pumpkins?
9. True or false: Pumpkins should be planted in direct sunlight.
10. How do you know it's time to harvest your pumpkins?

Memory Assessment

Needs improvement: Answered 1-2 questions correctly

Average: Answered 3-4 questions correctly

Good: Answered 5-6 questions correctly

Very good: Answered 7-8 questions correctly

Excellent: Answered 9-10 questions correctly

Set Three: How to Make Eggnog

Eggnog

6 eggs, separated   Nutmeg
Pinch salt   1 quart milk
½ cup sugar   ¾ cup rum
Scant 1 teaspoon vanilla

Beat egg yolks with salt; gradually add sugar, and beat until thick. Add vanilla and a little nutmeg to taste. Add milk and rum. Beat egg whites until they are stiff. Fold stiffly beaten egg whites in and let stand. Mix before serving.

Answer the following questions. (Answers are on page 147.)

1. What is the first thing you must do with the eggs?
2. What liquor will be used?
3. How many eggs are required?
4. What ingredient will you combine with the beaten egg yolks?
5. What flavorings are required?
6. What is the last ingredient to be added?

Memory Assessment
Needs improvement: Answered 1-2 questions correctly

Average: Answered 3 questions correctly

Good: Answered 4 questions correctly

Very good: Answered 5 questions correctly

Excellent: Answered 6 questions correctly

Memory Chargers

1. Make it a point each day to experience something new through active observation.

   Going for a walk along your normal route? Find something you never noticed before.

   Driving to work? Discover a new route to or from your workplace

   Going shopping? Talk to someone with whom you would not normally converse. Engage in brief conversation with the checkout clerk at the supermarket. Find out one interesting fact about the person.

   Listen for the sounds of the season. What does the rain sound like as it hits the pavement or drops into the ocean? Does snow really fall silently?

   Do something physically different each day. Try eating a meal with chopsticks. Brush your teeth with your nondominant hand. Fold your arms in the opposite direction from your norm.

2. Identify the top three to five items you typically misplace (e.g., keys, glasses, cell phone, etc.). Make a point of "seeing," "hearing," or "feeling" where you put the object down. Never put the object down again without seeing, hearing, or feeling its location.

   See yourself put the yellow receipt in the zipper compartment of your brown wallet.

   Hear the sound of the car keys as they drop on the tile of the kitchen counter.

   Feel the cell phone drop in the pocket of your coat.

3. When waiting in long lines, rather than getting bored or frustrated, take on the role of a crime scene detective. Imagine that a crime is about to be committed (e.g., a kidnapping or a robbery) and you will be called on to report the details of the scene. What do you see, hear, smell, feel, and so forth?

Make an Association

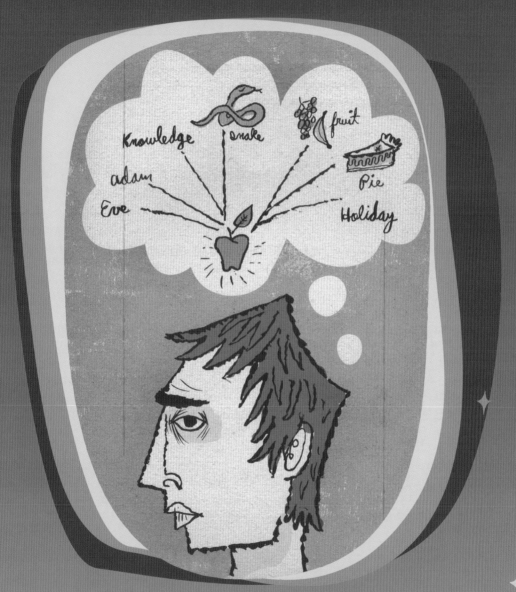

We remember by association. Every piece of information in our memory is connected to other pieces in some way or another.

—Kevin Jay North, *How to Improve Your Memory,* online tutorial

A Is for "Association"

An A+ memory consists of one part attention and one part association. Association involves connecting and associating the information to be remembered with what the brain already knows. All memory is based on association, whether unconscious or conscious. Unconscious associations are continually triggering memories. A song on the radio can trigger the memory of an old lover. The smell of wet pine needles may remind you of summer camp. Conscious associations are often used in school as memory aids. If you took music lessons, you probably learned to associate the treble clef notes of E, G, B, D, and F with the sentence "Every good boy does fine." To remember personal identification codes, we often use familiar associations such as a pet's name or a relative's birthday. Association techniques draw on the visual, auditory, and experiential learning styles you were introduced to in Lesson Two.

Visual Associations

Visual associations turn information you are trying to remember into mental images. For instance, to remember Mr. Bernhart's name you might associate the name with the image of a burning red heart. To remember that you parked your car in row 3B, Purple Zone, you might picture three purple bumblebees buzzing around your car.

Verbal Associations

Verbal associations draw on simple sound patterns (such as rhymes and alliteration) and other verbal reinforcers such as acronyms and acrostics. To remember to pick up your friend at 2 P.M., you might create this simple rhyme: Pick up Sue at two or she'll be blue. Combining visual and verbal associations provides even more memory glue. Adding this picture to your rhyme makes the memory more vivid. Picture Sue dripping in blue paint from head to foot.

Experiential Associations

Experiential associations utilize dynamic action-oriented connections, often with a wacky or humorous aspect. To remember that your insurance agent has a new office on the corner of Dogwood Street and Cherry Lane, you might create a mental scene in which the cartoon dog Scooby-Doo is catching cherries in his open mouth as they drop from a tree.

In the following memory games, you'll use visual, auditory, and experiential associations to power up for an A+ memory.

It Starts with the Letter . . .

Memory Skills:
Association

Memory Process:
Recall

Challenge Level:

How to Play

One way the brain stores names is through first-letter association. In this game, you will be asked to recall the names of people, places, and things using first-letter association. The object of the game is to see how quickly you can come up with a name using the first-letter association clue. Keep track of the total time it takes you to complete the game.

A B C

Name the item that begins with each letter.

1. Name a vegetable beginning with the letter *S*.
2. Name a fruit beginning with the letter *P*.
3. Name a fish beginning with the letter *T*.
4. Name a bird beginning with the letter *R*.
5. Name a flower beginning with the letter *D*.
6. Name a country beginning with the letter *I*.
7. Name a movie star beginning with the letter *C*.
8. Name an animal beginning with the letter *B*.
9. Name a U.S. state beginning with the letter *L*.
10. Name a tree beginning with the letter *O*.
11. Name a tool beginning with the letter *H*.
12. Name a cereal brand beginning with the letter *K*.
13. Name a food beginning with the letter *M*.
14. Name a breed of dog beginning with the letter *S*.
15. Name a body of water beginning with the letter *A*.

Memory Booster

Relax and have fun. Anxiety blocks memory processes.

It Ends with the Letter . . .

How to Play

This game is a variation of the previous game. The object of the game is to identify names of people, places, and things using *last*-letter association. Since the brain does not typically store and retrieve names in this fashion, you will experience a greater level of challenge. The purpose of this exercise is not to frustrate you, but rather to demonstrate the importance of creating meaningful and memorable associations that complement the brain's own memory processes. Keep track of the total time it takes to complete this game. Compare your completion time for this game with your time for the previous game. If you are like most people, you will find first-letter association to be a more reliable and efficient memory tool.

Name the item that ends with each letter.

1. Name a vegetable ending with the letter *H*.
2. Name a fruit ending with the letter *E*.
3. Name a fish ending with the letter *K*.
4. Name a bird ending with the letter *T*.
5. Name a flower ending with the letter *A*.
6. Name a country ending with the letter *D*.
7. Name a movie star ending with the letter *S*.
8. Name a working animal ending with the letter *E*.
9. Name a an article of clothing ending with the letter *T*.
10. Name a tree ending with the letter *M*.
11. Name a tool ending with the letter *R*.
12. Name an ice cream flavor ending with the letter *Y*.
13. Name a food ending with the letter *I*.
14. Name a breed of dog ending with the letter *R*.
15. Name a color ending with the letter *E*.

Memory Booster

If you get stuck, move on to the next item. Then review the list a second time to try to complete items you skipped.

Acronyms and Acrostics

Memory Skills:
Association
Memory Process:
Recognition and Recall
Challenge Level:

How to Play

Acronyms and acrostics use verbal associations to help us remember information better. Acronyms are created by turning the first letters of the items to be remembered into familiar words or verbal sounds. The well-known acronym for Mothers Against Drunk Driving is MADD. In school, many of us learned the acronym HOMES for the Great Lakes of the United States: Huron, Ontario, Michigan, Erie, and Superior.

To create an acrostic, use the first letters of the items you wish to remember to form a memorable phrase or sentence. An acrostic sentence kids use in science classes to help remember the order of living things is "King Phil came over for the gumbo special," which stands for kingdom, phylum, class, order, genus, species.

In this game, you will be presented with short lists of items to be remembered. Use the first letter of each word in the list to create either an acronym (word) or acrostic (sentence). If the order of the items is irrelevant, you can rearrange the items to help you create the most meaningful and memorable acronym or acrostic. Check your responses against the sample responses in the answer key on page 147–148.

1. Life cycle of a butterfly:
   egg
   larva
   pupa
   adult

2. Colors of the rainbow:
   red
   orange
   yellow
   green
   blue
   indigo
   violet

3. How to reduce the pain and swelling resulting from a sprain or strain:
   elevate
   ice
   compress
   rest

4. Steps for operating a home fire extinguisher:
   Pull pin from extinguisher handle.
   Aim extinguisher at base of fire.
   Squeeze the handle.
   Sweep the fire again at the base.

5. Grocery List:
   pears
   apples
   peaches
   cherries

6. Grocery List:
   turnips
   avocado
   radishes
   carrots

7. Errands:
   library
   cleaners

   bank
   optometrist

8. Seven Deadly Sins:
   pride
   envy
   gluttony
   lust
   anger
   greed
   sloth

9. Members of a business team:
   Angela
   Margaret
   Eddie
   Dennis

10. Members of a choral group:
    soprano
    alto
    tenor
    bass

Soft or Hard?

How to Play

In this game you are asked to categorize each word listed as something soft or something hard. Sorting items in a list by common category ties them together and helps us to remember the items better. Read each word below, one at a time, and think about which category it belongs in. Then see how many words you can remember associated with the memory categories "soft" and "hard." Tactile triggers such as "soft" and "hard" draw on the strengths of an experiential learner.

Read each word, and then ask yourself the question, Would this word be hard or soft to the touch?

1. Water
2. Rock
3. Shoe
4. Feather
5. Cotton
6. Horseshoe
7. Balloon
8. Baby
9. Telephone
10. Tree

Now cover the list and write down all the words you remember under the association categories "soft" and "hard" on a separate piece of paper.

Memory Assessment

Needs improvement: Recalled 1-2 words

Average: Recalled 3-4 words

Good: Recalled 5-6 words

Very good: Recalled 7-8 words

Excellent: Recalled 9-10 words

Memory Booster

You can employ a combination of learning styles to reinforce the "soft" and "hard" word associations. Visualize the delicate formation of the soft words and the solid formation of the hard words. Imagine you are touching each item. Try to feel its softness or hardness. Speak the "soft" words in a whisper and the "hard" words in a shout.

Pleasant or Unpleasant?

How to Play

In this game you are asked to categorize each word listed as something pleasant or something unpleasant. Read each word below, one at a time, and think about which category it belongs in. Then see how many words you can remember associated with the memory categories "pleasant" and "unpleasant."

Read each word, and then ask yourself the question, Would this word be pleasant or unpleasant in a hurricane?

1. Water
2. Shelter
3. Blanket
4. Wind
5. Electricity
6. Trees
7. Radio
8. Boat
9. School
10. Telephone

Now cover the list and write down all the words you can remember under the association categories "pleasant" and "unpleasant" on a separate piece of paper.

Memory Assessment

Needs improvement:	Recalled 1–2 words
Average:	Recalled 3–4 words
Good:	Recalled 5–6 words
Very good:	Recalled 7–8 words
Excellent:	Recalled 9–10 words

Memory Booster

You can employ a combination of learning styles to reinforce the "pleasant" and "unpleasant" associations. Imagine what the "pleasant" and "unpleasant" items would feel like, look like, or sound like in the middle of a hurricane. For example, what would it feel like to be drenched with cold ocean water? What would it feel like to be wrapped in a soft, warm blanket? What would the wind sound like? What would a boat on the ocean look like? Memories with a strong emotional connection are some of the most secure and long-lasting memories.

People Pictures

How to Play

Many people's given names have built-in meaning that can be used to create a memory association. Match each name in column A with its image association in column B. (See page 148 for answers.)

Names	Image
1. Ms. Hilliard	A. Bouquet of flowers
2. Mr. Butler	B. Pitcher of cream
3. Ms. Juliano	C. Quacking duck
4. Mr. Schwimmer	D. Golden goblet
5. Ms. Huffington	E. Fancy chocolates
6. Dr. Krebsrach	F. Singing choir
7. Ms. Maguire	G. British manservant
8. Mr. Knickerbacker	H. Keg of beer
9. Ms. Albright	I. Lady out of breath
10. Mr. Mason	J. Pony ride
11. Ms. Gianelli	K. Olympic swimmer
12. Mr. Mendoza	L. Hilly yard
13. Ms. Flores	M. Farmer bailing hay
14. Mr. Hayman	N. Crab on rock
15. Ms. Angellini	O. Chain around knee
16. Mr. Goldstein	P. Angel hair pasta
17. Ms. Cheney	Q Men taking siesta
18. Mr. Trotter	R. Ring through nose
19. Mr. Kareem	S. Rays of sunlight
20. Ms. Quackenboss	T. Stone wall

Memory Booster

If a name does not immediately conjure up a mental picture, try breaking the name into syllables. Often you can find an image in one or more of the syllables that will serve as a memory hook. If that does not work, try using an auditory learning style. Perhaps one or more of the syllables rhymes with a picture word. For example, the name Pinelli rhymes with "jelly."

Memory Assessment

Average: Matched 25 percent correctly

Good: Matched 50 percent correctly

Very good: Matched 75 percent correctly

Excellent: Matched 100 percent correctly

Side by Side

How to Play

You will be presented with several pairs of words. Each pair will consist of an italicized word and a capitalized word. Create a memorable association between the two that will help you to remember the capitalized word. You'll be asked to remember more words, and the correlation between the paired words will be less obvious.

Set One

Read each pair of words, focusing on remembering the capitalized word. Then look at the next page.

floor   DUST

laundry   SOAP

light   BULB

whistle   WIND

swift   RUN

command   ARMY

beat   TENNIS

needle   SCRATCH

blow   BUBBLE

knife   MEAT

ink   COMPUTER

puppy   SOFT

Memory Booster

The more colorful, dynamic, and emotional (scary, funny, sad, etc.) the association, the stronger the memory link. Try adding a personal link by putting yourself in the association. For example, if the word pair is "*ski*" and "BATHING SUIT," imagine yourself spring skiing in the melting snow of the Alps wearing nothing but a bathing suit and sunglasses.

Next to each italicized word, write the capitalized word that is paired with it on the previous page.

floor _____

laundry _____

light _____

whistle _____

swift _____

command _____

beat _____

needle _____

blow _____

knife _____

ink _____

puppy _____

Memory Assessment

Needs improvement: Remembered 1–3 words

Average: Remembered 4–5 words

Good: Remembered 6–7 words

Very good: Remembered 8–9 words

Excellent: Remembered 10–12 words

Set Two

Read each pair of words, focusing on remembering the capitalized words. Then go to the next page.

ice   FISH

cloth   NAPKIN

man   PRIEST

animal   FOREST

need   MONEY

jar   HAMMER

head   BUSINESS

tooth   YELLOW

cliff   BAND-AID

hospital   QUIET

faint   HOT

sugar   TEA

paper clip   HOLD

girl   PRINCESS

lost   KEYS

Next to each italicized word, write the capitalized word that is paired with it on the previous page.

ice _____

cloth _____

man _____

animal _____

need _____

jar _____

head _____

tooth _____

cliff _____

hospital _____

faint _____

sugar _____

paper clip _____

girl _____

lost _____

Set Three

Read each pair of words, focusing on remembering the capitalized word. Then go to the next page.

barber   GRASS

hug   SNAKE

sand   SALTY

smoke   MIRROR

rainbow   PRETTY

squash   BUG

white   SILK

cherish   RING

claw   BEAR

cold   PENCIL

bright   BALL

lopsided   BIKE

crushed   LIQUID

quiet   SNOW

tall   ANT

black   MOON

bold   MONKEY

slippery   HOUSE

restful   PLAY

musical   CLOUD

Next to each italicized word, write the capitalized word that is paired with it on the previous page.

barber _____

hug _____

sand _____

smoke _____

rainbow _____

squash _____

white _____

cherish _____

claw _____

cold _____

bright _____

lopsided _____

crushed _____

quiet _____

tall _____

black _____

bold _____

slippery _____

restful _____

musical _____

Memory Assessment

Needs improvement: Remembered 1-5 words

Average: Remembered 6-10 words

Good: Remembered 11-13 words

Very good: Remembered 14-16 words

Excellent: Remembered 17-20 words

Wacky Pairs

Memory Skills:
Association
Memory Process:
Recognition
Challenge Level:

How to Play

Now that you've practiced remembering through associations, you can progress to the next level of challenge. In this game, you'll be given pairs of words that, on the surface, appear to have no connection with each other. Study each pair of seemingly unrelated words. Spend up to one minute per pair playing with different associations that will connect the words. Then move on to the next pair. Use your imagination to connect each pair of words in as many ways as possible. Then go to the next page.

Study the word pairs below and form associations.

BRICK	TREE	CLOUD	TEAPOT
CARRIAGE	BABY	SCISSORS	BIRD
MEADOW	BARN	GYPSY	APPLE
PAINTBRUSH	TEACHER	RABBIT	BRIEFCASE
SPAGHETTI	PIPE	WINDMILL	SWIMMER
TRAIN	CAMERA	STAR	OCEAN

Memory Booster

Visualize the paired words together in a dynamic and colorful interaction. See the word images merging or crashing into each other. Add an emotional element to the interaction to make it either funny or frightening. Memories with an emotional association have more memory glue. For the word pair "dog" and "glass," a vivid and emotional interaction might involve a tiny white puppy cutting its soft paw on a piece of jagged, broken glass. A humorous association might be a fancy white French poodle with a rhinestone collar, strutting down the street in designer sunglasses.

Draw lines to connect the words on the left with their original counterparts on the right. Check your matches against the original pairings on the preceding page.

BRICK	TEACHER
CARRIAGE	SPAGHETTI
TREE	STAR
TEAPOT	BABY
BIRD	SWIMMER
MEADOW	CLOUD
GYPSY	TRAIN
RABBIT	OCEAN
APPLE	PAINTBRUSH
PIPE	BRIEFCASE
CAMERA	SCISSORS
WINDMILL	BARN

Memory Assessment

Needs improvement: Matched 1–3 pairs

Average: Matched 4–5 pairs

Good: Matched 6–7 pairs

Very good: Matched 8–9 pairs

Excellent: Matched 10–12 pairs

Tell Me a Story

How to Play

In the following two sets of games, you will use the storybook memory method (see Memory Booster) to help you remember a list of unrelated words.

Set One

Use the storybook association method to help you remember the list of words at right. After you have mentally joined the words together in a mini-story, cover the words. Then, on a piece of scrap paper, write down all the words you can remember.

Flower
Party hat
Guitar
Jogger
Glasses
Queen
Dog

Memory Assessment

Needs improvement: Recalled 1–3 items

Average: Recalled 4 items

Good: Recalled 5 items

Very good: Recalled 6 items

Excellent: Recalled 7 items

Memory Booster

To boost your memory, shorten the number of individual items to be remembered by *connecting* them together in a mini-story. Make the items come alive in your story by using drama or humor. For instance, if the items to be remembered include a telephone, lipstick, and a mirror, your mini–story line might describe a woman on a dark and stormy night writing a *telephone* number she just received from the operator in red *lipstick* on her *mirror*.

Set Two

Use the storybook association method to help you remember the list of words below. The list represents items you will take on your upcoming hiking trip. After you have mental-ly joined the words together in a mini-story, cover the words. Then, on a piece of scrap paper, write down all the words you can remember.

Binoculars

Walking stick

Suntan lotion

Bug spray

Your hunting dog, Rufus

Hiking boots

Fishing rod

Worms

Your little brother, Ben

Memory Assessment

Needs improvement: Recalled 1–3 items

Average: Recalled 4 items

Good: Recalled 5 items

Very good: Recalled 6 items

Excellent: Recalled 7–9 items

Common Category

How to Play

Study the following picture collages for 3 minutes each. One collage features foods and the other features wildlife. Look for ways to group the items by common category. For instance, foods might be grouped and categorized by the major food groups or by taste (e.g., sweet or sour). Animals might be grouped and categorized by species or their natural habitat. Try to remember the items in each picture collage by associating them with their common category. Then cover the picture collage. Write down the categories you created, and then the items in each category.

Set One

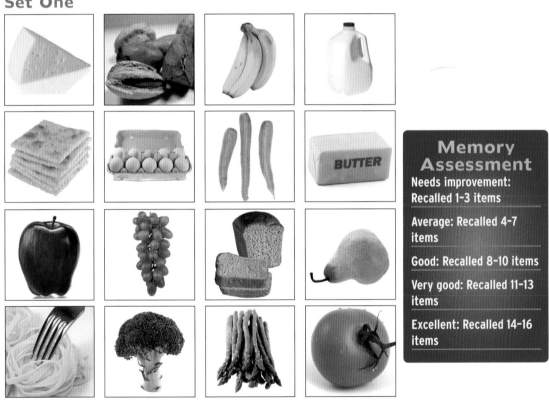

Memory Assessment

Needs improvement: Recalled 1–3 items

Average: Recalled 4–7 items

Good: Recalled 8–10 items

Very good: Recalled 11–13 items

Excellent: Recalled 14–16 items

Memory Booster

Categorization is an association memory technique that allows the brain to link items or facts to be remembered by common groupings. The category serves as a memory-encoding device that boosts memory organization, storage, and recall.

Set Two

Study the items in the collage for 3 minutes. Look for ways to group the items by common category. Then cover all the items. Write down the categories you remember, and then the items in each category.

What's It Called?

How to Play

Place names often have built-in visual imagery, making them fun and easy to remember. "Magnolia Street" is easy to picture when associated with the beautiful white flower of the same name. "Brookline Village" could be pictured as a stream of water forming a straight line through the center of a row of stores. Below is a list of names of real places. Study the list for up to 3 minutes. Then go to the next page.

1. Indian Ridge Country Club

2. Parker House Restaurant

3. Diamond Optical Eyewear

4. Corner of Elm Street and Bay View

5. American Rental Car

6. The Kittery Mall

7. High Plain Elementary School

8. Harmony Parkway

9. Jubilee Movie Plaza

10. Exit onto Baker Street

11. Children's Hospital

12. Deerfield Academy

Memory Booster

Drawing on a visual learning style, look for imagery built into each name. Try to create images that are colorful, dynamic, and humorous.

Write down the proper name that correlates with each place.

1. Country Club _____

2. Restaurant _____

3. Eyewear _____

4. Corner Streets _____

5. Rental Car _____

6. Mall _____

7. Elementary School _____

8. Parkway _____

9. Movie Plaza _____

10. Street Exit _____

11. Hospital _____

12. Academy _____

What's My Name?

Memory Skills:
Association

Memory Process:
Recall

Challenge Level:

How to Play

In this game you will be presented with the faces and names of nine people. Study the faces and their associated names for 3 minutes, and then go to the next page. As you study the names and faces, look for ways to create a memory association between the person's name and the person's face.

Bernard

Lily

Caesar

Isabella

Nicholas

Ashley

Harry

Faith

Abbey

Memory Booster

The key to remembering names is being able to connect the name with the face. To do this, some memory experts suggest a two-pronged approach. First create a memory hook for the name using one of the techniques described in the previous two Memory Boosters. Then look for creative ways to connect the name to a dominant facial feature. Perhaps you've just met someone named Ryan. Using a quick rhyming technique you come up with the memory hook, "Ryan the Lion." Now suppose that Ryan has bushy, yellow hair, reminding you of a lion's mane. Visually connect your two memory hooks. Picture a lion resting in Ryan's hair.

State the name that goes with each face. Use the initial clues to help you.

A   L   C

A   H   B

N   F   I

Memory Assessment

Needs improvement: Recalled 1-2 names

Average: Recalled 3-4 names

Good: Recalled 5-6 names

Very good: Recalled 7-8 names

Excellent: Recalled 9 names

Number Pictures

How to Play

Associating numbers with the image they look like can help you better remember the important numbers in your life, such as street addresses, security codes, telephone numbers, highway exits, bank accounts, and record locators. Memorize the number-image code below. Then go to the next page.

Number and Image Picture

0 = egg

1 = candle

2 = swan

3 = bird

4 = sailboat

5 = slide

6 = snake

7 = cliff edge

8 = snowman

9 = balloon

Memory Booster

Turn numbers into the images they look like. For instance, the number 81 looks like a snowman holding a candle.

Answer the following questions to test your recall of the number-image code. To check your responses, review the code on the previous page.

1. What two-digit number is represented by a sailboat and a balloon?

2. What two-digit number is represented by a snake and a swan?

3. What two-digit number is represented by a cliff edge and a slide?

4. What three-digit number is represented by a candle, a snowman, and bird?

5. What four-digit number is represented by a slide, egg, snake, and sailboat?

6. What number pictures correlate with the address of your home?

7. What number pictures correlate with your license plate?

8. What number pictures correlate with your birthday?

9. What number pictures correlate with the time of day it is right now?

10. What number pictures correlate with your telephone number?

Memory Assessment
Needs improvement: Gave 1-3 correct responses

Average: Gave 4-5 correct responses

Good: Gave 6-7 correct responses

Very good: Gave 8-9 correct responses

Excellent: Gave 10 correct responses

Name Game

How to Play

In this game you will be presented with a list of people's first names. Your challenge is to devise a memory association for each name using one or more of the ten techniques highlighted in the Memory Booster below.

Write each name on a piece of scrap paper. Next to each name, write your memory-boosting association. When you have finished, cover the names and use the associations to recall each one.

Names

Heather

Rodney

Candice

Forester

Carmella

Abdul

Angelina

Fernando

Brunetta

Sherwood

Memory Assessment

Needs improvement: Recalled 1-3 names

Average: Recalled 4-5 names

Good: Recalled 6-7 names

Very good: Recalled 8-9 names

Excellent: Recalled 10 names

Memory Booster

Not remembering names is one of the most common memory complaints, next to misplacing common objects such as keys and glasses. Remembering names of new acquaintances upon introduction involves four key steps: (1) Pay attention to the name when you are introduced; (2) repeat the name in conversation a minimum of three times; (3) mentally write the name in big bright letters on your mind's blackboard; and (4) create a meaningful memory hook using one or more of these popular association techniques:

• Same name as someone you know (Aunt Julia, Cousin Henry)

• Same name as a famous person (Clinton, Moses, Oprah)

• Same name as an occupation (Singer, Gardner, Carpenter, Butler)

• Same name as an animal (Fox, Swan)

• Same name as a flower or season (April, Rose)

• Same name as a famous brand (Campbell, Ford)

• Name with built-in imagery (Petski = Dog on skis; Greenberg = Head of lettuce)

• Name with obvious language translation (Morgenstern = German for "morning star")

• Name linked with dominant feature (Tall Tom)

• Name rhyme (Juliana Banana)

Memory Chargers

Have fun playing these memory association games with friends and family.

1. **License Plate Game**
Look for ways to convert license plate letters and numbers into memorable associations.
Example: License plate BOP-221 = Little Bo (BO) Peep (P) tends two swans (22) with a rod (1).

2. **Left-Right Direction Game**
Convert left-right directions into a memorable sentence in which each word begins with *L* (left) or *R* (right).
Example: Take a left on Woolbright, left on Military, right on Boynton, and a left into the mall. Convert *left*, *left*, *right*, *left* into a sentence: "Lucky Louie Rocks Louisville."

3. Turn street addresses and highway exit numbers into memorable picture images. Make up your own number-picture association code.
Example: Highway exit 24 to the beaches = A swan (2) following a sailboat (4).

4. Use rhymes and simple tunes to help you remember information.
Example: Take exit 24 because there are no more.
Example: Try singing the alphabet backward to "Twinkle, Twinkle, Little Star."

5. Turn lists of errands into memorable acronyms or acrostics.
Example: Today's errands: cleaners, bank, pharmacy, library = "The clever banker picks the lock."

Answer Key

Colorful Stories (pages 30–37)

Story One
Question:
Bach
Colors:
1. Gray
2. Ebony
3. Golden
4. Red
5. Brown

Story Two
Question:
Washing laundry
Colors:
1. Black
2. Green
3. Red
4. Blue
5. Brown

Story Three
Question:
Air France
Colors:
1. White
2. Blue
3. Pink
4. Gray
5. Red

Story Four
Question:
Fairlee, Vermont
Colors:
1. Green
2. White
3. Blue
4. Azure
5. Gray

Story Five
Question:
Victorian
Colors:
1. Yellow
2. Silver
3. Mahogany
4. Rose
5. Green
6. Auburn
7. China blue

Story Six
Question:
Benches
Colors:
1. Blue
2. Purple
3. Gray
4. Red
5. Brown
6. Black
7. Golden

Story Seven
Question:
County Clare
Colors:
1. Red
2. Green
3. Orange
4. Blue
5. Dark brown
6. Black
7. White

Television Jingles (page 59)
1. Rice Krispies cereal
2. Exxon gasoline
3. Mounds and Almond Joy candy
4. Wheaties cereal
5. Miller
6. Preference hair color by L'Oréal
7. CNN
8. Folgers coffee
9. Dr. Pepper soft drink
10. Frosted Flakes
11. Doublemint chewing gum
12. Hellmann's mayonnaise
13. Sara Lee
14. Campbell's soup
15. Green Giant
16. Hallmark greeting cards
17. Star-Kist tuna
18. Alka-Seltzer
19. Chiffon margarine
20. Kentucky Fried Chicken
21. McDonald's
22. NBC television
23. Coke
24. Capital One credit card
25. Chevrolet
26. United Airlines
27. U.S. Army
28. Verizon Wireless
29. Burger King
30. Brylcreem

Movie Mania (pages 60–61)
1. *Gone with the Wind*
2. *The Godfather*
3. *Moonstruck*
4. *The Wizard of Oz*
5. *Casablanca*
6. *Sudden Impact*
7. *Star Wars*
8. *Bonnie and Clyde*
9. *Jerry Maguire*
10. *Apocalypse Now*
11. *E.T. The Extra-Terrestrial*
12. *The Silence of the Lambs*
13. *Jaws*
14. *The Wizard of Oz*
15. *Jerry Maguire*
16. *Gone with the Wind*
17 *When Harry Met Sally*
18. *Titanic*
19. *Field of Dreams*
20. *Forrest Gump*
21. *Apollo 13*
22. *The Graduate*
23. *Casablanca*
24. *Terminator 2: Judgment Day*
25. *Dead Poets Society*
26. *Dirty Dancing*

27. *Pirates of the Caribbean: The Black Pearl*
28. *Knute Rockne, All American*
29. *Rocky*
30. *The Sixth Sense*

Words of Wisdom
(pages 62–63)
1. Bush
2. Link
3. Keeps
4. Moss
5. Nine
6. Spots
7. Away
8. Fonder
9. Words
10. End
11. War
12. Gold
13. Well
14. Fast
15. Deep
16. Never
17. Together
18. Water
19. Beholder
20. Home
21. Pay
22. Cat
23. Hatch
24. Face
25. Basket
26. Public
27. Done
28. Teacher
29. Due
30. Themselves

31. Neighbors
32. Contempt
33. Weepers
34. Alike
35. Policy
36. Bliss
37. Milk
38. Tango
39. Live
40. Medicine
41. Lie
42. Beware
43. Cherries
44. Son
45. Leap
46. All
47. Evil
48. Taxes
49. Success
50. Gained
51. Invention
52. News
53. Gain
54. Hard
55. Twice
56. Perfect
57. Believing
58. Golden
59. Deep
60. Hot
61. Worm
62. Free
63. Thieves
64. Numbers
65. Means
66. Hardest
67. Fence
68. Want
69. Eating
70. Story
71. Fire

72. Divine
73. Day
74. Broth
75. Fool
76. No one
77. Stones
78. Wounds
79. One
80. Crowd
81. Life
82. Reward
83. Nothing
84. Way
85. Cover

Who Am I?
(pages 64–65)
1. Amelia Earhart
2. Al Capone
3. Aretha Franklin
4. Florence Nightingale
5. Jesse Jackson
6. Helen Keller
7. LeAnn Rimes
8. Mahatma Gandhi
9. Rosa Parks
10. Eminem
11. Julia Child
12. Cesar Chavez
13. Neil Armstrong
14. Grace Kelly
15. Marquis de Sade
16. Babe Ruth
17. Julie Andrews
18. Prophet Muhammad
19. Thurgood Marshall
20. Maria Sharapova

What Am I
(page 66)
1. Soccer
2. Snorkel
3. Hypothermia
4. Stanza
5. Passport
6. Lease
7. Patent
8. Trampoline
9. Venom
10. Allergy
11. Cadaver
12. Embroidery
13. Sorbet

Famous Quotations
(page 67)
1. F
2. O
3. N
4. L
5. K
6. I
7. J
8. M
9. E
10. G
11. B
12. D
13. C
14. H
15. A

Around the World (pages 68–69)
1. J
2. K
3. L

4. N	14. C	**Famous Places**	9. J
5. O	15. T	(page 70)	10. I
6. Ɛ	16. D	1. N	11. K
7. P	17. F	2. Ɛ	12. H
8. Q	18. G	3. O	13. C
9. H	19. R	4. D	14. F
10. B	20. S	5. B	15. G
11. A		6. R	16. Q
12. I		7. L	17. P
13. M		8. M	18. A

What Do You Know? (page 71)

1. A. True. According to the American Federation for Aging Research, most of us will experience mild memory problems as we age owing to some brain cell loss and brain shrinkage. However, for the majority of people, memory loss, while a nuisance, will not interfere with everyday living nor progress to a serious brain disease.

2. B. False. The brain is a dynamic organ capable of regeneration at any age. In a clinical study, seniors who participated in a program of planned mental exercises over a period of several weeks showed lasting gains in memory and mental agility.

3. D. None of the above. Memory glitches such as these can happen to anyone at any age. They tend to happen more frequently when we are stressed, tired, or multitasking.

4. D. Needing extra time to do calculations in your head. As we age, processing speed slows down and we may find it takes just a little longer to perform some mental functions. Items A, B, and C are signs of serious mental problems and should be checked out immediately by a medical doctor. If taken early, there are medicines that can slow down the progress of certain brain diseases.

5. A. True. Short-term memory is the first mental process noticeably affected by Alzheimer's disease. Some early symptoms include: (1) doing the same task over and over again; (2) repeating the same story over and over again; (3) asking the same question many times; (4) forgetting that you just performed an activity or task.

6. D. All of the above. There are many reversible medical conditions that cause temporary memory loss. This is why it is so important to seek medical help if you are having memory problems that interfere with daily living. Many women complain of memory problems during certain stages of their lives when they experience hormonal imbalances, such as during pregnancy, perimenopause, and menopause.

7. A. True. Heavy alcohol use kills brain cells and impairs memory. Conversely, recent studies have shown that a glass of wine a day can help improve brain function by opening up blood vessels, thereby increasing blood flow to the brain.

8. C. Coffee. In a recent clinical study, seniors who had a cup of coffee prior to engaging in mental exercises fared better than those who did not consume the coffee.

9. B. Multitasking. Short-term memory is increasingly susceptible to interference and disruption as we age. Multitasking is a major source of interference that drains the brain, reducing our ability

to focus in the moment. You can't remember what you don't pay attention to in the first place. Additionally, multitasking in an office environment has been shown to reduce the quality of the work being performed.

10. B. False. Only 10 percent of the population over age sixty-five show signs of Alzheimer's disease, while 50 percent of the population over age eighty-five are at risk for the disease. However, because the brain is a resilient organ capable of regeneration, the things you do today, and as you continue to age, to build a better brain can help slow down and ward off dementia.

11. A. Not getting a good night's sleep. Sleep is critical to memory storage and consolidation. Clinical studies show that when we sleep, memories are hardwired into the brain. People who get a good night's sleep (eight hours a night) are also more likely to be able to come up with creative solutions to problems.

12. D. All of the above. Lifestyle factors trump genetics when it comes to a sharper memory and a better brain. "Getting your sneakers moving" is the number one lifestyle factor when it comes to brain health. When you engage in aerobic exercise, you increase blood flow to your vital organs, bringing with it important nutrients that feed and fuel the brain.

Autopilot
(page 76)
Note: Answers to questions based on personal information are not listed below.
1. Abraham Lincoln
2. Octagon (eight sides)
3. Orange
5. Green, yellow, red
6. Orange and pink
8. Left
9. Flashing lights and stop-sign arm
10. Fifty-two
11. Six
12. Two
14. Above
15. Diagonal

Unfocused Reader (page 77)
Each phrase has a repeated word, making the sentences grammatically incorrect.

Focused Reader
(pages 78–79)
Excerpt One
1. Cave
2. Gold
3. One dollar
4. Widow Douglas
5. Rags and sugar-hogshead
6. To start a band of robbers

Excerpt Two
1. 1632
2. Ancient
3. House-education and country free-school
4. Law
5. Misery
6. Almost a year
7. London
8. Nothing
9. Father of a companion
10. No word

Compare and Contrast (pages 80–85)
Jungle Mania
1. Monkey eyes closed
2. Top left pink butterfly antennae
3. Snake skin pattern
4. Snake fangs/toungue
5. Flying insect direction
6. Orange butterfly wing pattern
7. Leaf missing by white bird
8. White bird crown
9. Colored parrot feet
10. Caterpillar below monkey

Flower Garden
1. Dark clouds
2. Makeup lips/cheek
3. Color pattern on dress
4. Bracelet missing
5. Tire/swing
6. Tree branches
7. Caterpillar below butterfly
8. Flower with brown leaf moved to left side
9. Watering can spout holes
10. Pond missing

Fish Tank
1. Hook direction
2. Fish bubbles much less
3. Current pattern direction near hook
4. Jelly fish tentacles

5. Top purple fish pattern
6. Upper right orange fish tail
7. Two more seaweed strands
8. Extra shell/sand dollar
9. Bottom little fish color and fin missing
10. Bottom left of three corals color change

Mixed-Bag Patterns (pages 97–100)
Set One
1. 8
2. K
3. Square
4. Four
5. 9
6. 5
7. B
8. Octagon
9. 1
10. M
11. Red
12. Blue

Set Two
1. 3
2. 6
3. Circle
4. 2
5. Four
6. 8
7. T
8. Pentagon

9. Three
10. 12
11. Black (or blue)
12. Blue (or red, purple, or orange)

Out and About
(see pages 101–108)
Scene One: On the Farm
1. Dog and mouse
2. No
3. Rooster
4. Rooster crowing and sun rising
5. Left
6. Fence
7. Rake
8. Feeding chickens
9. Corn
10. Dog

Scene Two: At the Beach
1. A man is wearing sandals
2. Palm tree leaning over, strong surf, hat blowing off woman's head, and loose newspaper flying up
3. Girl
4. Yes
5. 4
6. Starfish, shell, sand dollar
7. Two
8. Surfing and boating
9. Newspaper
10. Watermelon

Scene Three: City Slicker
1. Eight
2. Pet shop
3. Skateboard and bicycle
4. Fur coat and hat
5. Barking
6. Left
7. Two
8. Banana peel
9. Stop
10. Buildings and clouds

Scene Four: Central Park
1. To the lake
2. Two
3. No swimming!
4. Man playing checkers
5. Ponytails
6. Horse
7. Left
8. Reading a newspaper
9. Checkers
10. One

Make It; Grow It (pages 109–113)
Set One: How to Make Sweet Potato Casserole
1. Hot water, orange juice, and apricot liquid
2. Dried
3. ½ inch
4. Sweet potatoes, apricots, brown sugar

5. 375 degrees
6. 40 minutes
7. Marshmallows

Set Two: How to Grow Pumpkins
1. To keep them symmetrical
2. Compost tea or seaweed extract
3. Place boards under large pumpkins
4. Frost
5. Five feet in each direction
6. Fifteen feet in all directions
7. One to two inches
8. 6.0 or 6.8
9. True
10. Harvest after the vines have shriveled and died, but before the first hard freeze

Set Three: How to Make Eggnog
1. Beat egg yolks
2. Rum
3. Six
4. Salt
5. Vanilla and nutmeg
6. Stiffly beaten egg whites

Acronyms and Acrostics
(page 119)
Sample Responses
1. Elly likes purple ants.
2. Roy G. Biv
3. RICE

4. PASS
5. CAPP
6. CART
7. BLOC
8. Penny eats green licorice and green snails.
9. DAMƐ
10. STAB

People Pictures
(page 122)
1. L
2. G
3. R
4. K
5. I
6. N
7. F
8. H
9. S
10. T
11. Ɛ
12. Q
13. A
14. M
15. P
16. D
17. O
18. J
19. B
20. C

Bibliography

Keep Learning

Following is a list of author-recommended books with fun exercises and edifying information that will help you to keep your memory supercharged.

Chalton, Nicola. *Memory Power*. New York: Barnes and Noble, 2006.

Devanand, D.P. *The Memory Program*. Hoboken, NJ: Wiley, 2001.

Einstein, Gilles O., and Mark A. McDaniel. *Memory Fitness*. New Haven, CT: Yale University Press, 2004.

Fogler, Janet, and Lynn Stern. *Improving Your Memory*. Baltimore: John Hopkins University Press, 1994.

Gediman, Corinne L., with Francis M. Crinella. *Brainfit: 10 Minutes a Day for a Sharper Mind and Memory*. Nashville, TN: Rutledge Hill Press, 2005.

Gordon, Barry. *Intelligent Memory*. New York: Viking, 2003.

Green, Cynthia R. *Total Memory Workout*. New York: Bantam Books, 1999.

Lapp, Danielle C. *Don't Forget*. New York: McGraw-Hill, 1987.

Lapp, Danielle C. *Maximizing Your Memory Power*. Hauppauge, NY: Barrons Educational Series, 1998.

Noir, Michel, and Bernard Croisile. *Dental Floss for the Mind*. New York: McGraw-Hill, 2005.

Small, Gary. *The Memory Bible*. New York: Hyperion, 2002.

Small, Gary. *The Memory Prescription*. New York: Hyperion, 2005.

Roberts, Russell. *10 Days to a Sharper Memory*. New York: Warner Books, 2001.

Turkington, Carol. *12 Steps to a Better Memory*. New York: Macmillan, 1996.

Wetzel, Kathryn, and Kathleen Harmeyer. *Mind Games*. Albany, NY: Thompson Delmar Learning, 2000.

Photo Credits

© AP Images, pages:11 right, 12 right

© iStockphoto, pages: 11 left, 137 all except bottom right,138 all except center row far left

© Gettyimages, pages: 12 left, 13

© Shutterstock, pages: 16, 29, 31–36, 59–60, 68–69, 120, 125, 133–135, 137 bottom right, 138 center row far left

© United States Air Force, page: 75

Index

About the Authors

CORINNE LILLE GEDIMAN is an adult learning specialist and professional development consultant with 25 years of experience designing and facilitating learning experiences for corporate clients around the globe. She is a senior resource consultant with The Forum Corporation, an international training and consulting company, with offices in Boston, Hong Kong, and the United Kingdom. More recently, Ms. Gediman has been applying her expertise in adult learning to the field of neuroscience and brain training. Her mentor and collaborator is Dr. Francis Crinella, a recognized subject matter expert, researcher, and clinical professor in neuropsychology at the University of California at Irvine. By combining strengths, Ms.Gediman and Dr. Crinella are developing exciting new brain training programs that draw on adult learning principles and proven clinical science.

In partnership, Corinne Gediman and Dr. Crinella have previously authored *Brainfit: 10 Minutes a Day for a Sharper Mind and Memory* (Rutledge Hill Press). Ms. Gediman is a principal partner in a new company, Brainfit Inc., which develops and markets "train-your-brain" games for the online and downloadable markets (Internet, cell phones, BlackBerrys, etc.) Her Web site is www.brainfit.net. In addition to the development of books and games, Ms. Gediman is a sought-after speaker on cruise ships (Queen Mary II), resort spas (Canyon Ranch), and syndicated radio talk shows. She recently appeared on *Good Morning Miami*.

DR. FRANCIS MICHAEL CRINELLA is the Director of the Neuropsychology Laboratory and a Clinical Professor of neuropsychology at the University of California at Irvine. He is a highly respected neuropsychologist who has devoted his career to the study of brain function and brain plasticity. Dr. Crinella's history as a memory researcher dates back to 1966, when he began working with the great Bob Thompson at Louisiana State University. Thompson was a student of the father of American neuropsychology, Karl Lashley, who dedicated his life to searching for the memory "engram" (a protoplasmic alteration hypothesized to occur upon stimulation of living neural tissue and to account for memory). In addition to teaching and his clinical practice, Dr. Crinella has conducted numerous research studies and written many academic papers on brain plasticity, memory, and mental agility.